Jordans of the Pond

A History of
*The Family from the Jordan Pond House
On Mount Desert Island, Maine*

By
James D. Reeverts

Illustrations by Robert P. Kline

Watercolors by Thomas J. Reeverts

Published by American Publishing
ISBN 979-8-9877473-9-1

Reeverts, James D., 1957
1. Jordan Pond House. 2. Jordan Family History. 3. Mount Desert Island, Maine. 4. Acadia National Park. 5. Seal Harbor, Maine 6. Genealogy – George N. Jordan, Sr. 7. Travel – Downeast Maine.

Production Credits:
Cover Design: Hannah Linder Books
Interior Design: AtriTeX Technologies

Illustrations by Robert P. Kline
Watercolors by Thomas J. Reeverts

Library of Congress Cataloging-in-Publication Data
Reeverts, James D.
Jordans of the Pond: A History of the Family from the Jordan Pond House on Mount Desert Island, Maine / James D. Reeverts

Printed in the United States of America

DEDICATION

TO
Carolyn Mae Reeverts
In memory of her mother, Myra Jordan

Mom, I'll love you forever.
Thank you for the precious memories
of our trips to Seal Harbor and to Jordan Pond.
~JDR

CONTENTS

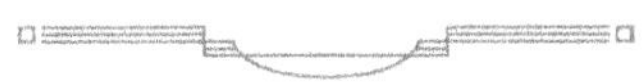

PREFACE

Much of the literature and signage referring to the Jordan Pond House, Acadia National Park's restaurant in Seal Harbor, Maine, recounts few details of either the vocation or the family life of those for whom it is named. Mount Desert Island historian Tim Garrity suggests, "Some things will be forever lost to antiquity." Even the Jordan family hailing from those who lived at the historic house knows little about the era of origin—1837-1879. While it predates the story of the restaurant, the Jordan history keeps its relevance as the roots of the lake's identity, if not the location itself. (This is part of the story of life on Mount Desert Island before it hosted a national park or became a notable favorite for summer residents.)

This Jordan family story took place mostly along the shores of the pond that bears their name. For as much as the narratives of other local families embody the bold and romantic notion of life in the 1800s, the Jordan's loss of land, loved ones, and livelihood unveils a different but prevalent reality amidst the era of growing island fame.

This history is primarily recounted from the records of the eldest Jordan brother, George, my great-great-grandfather. I have studied the island's history, traversed its hills and shorelines. Nothing awakened me more than when I realized his livelihood may have been the center of controversy. I knew the story of the Jordan family needed to be unearthed. The records, recollections, and discoveries are pieced together to form a reasonable account of life during the family's era at Jordan Pond. Some narrative embellishment is interspersed. However, all historical context and any creative imagination is designed to support the factual record. Readers are encouraged to enjoy other historical accounts of this and surrounding eras for a full appreciation of the dynamics and struggles of the early days on Mount Desert Island.

INTRODUCTION

"The Jordan Pond House began as a humble farmhouse built by George and John Jordan. A small apple orchard was planted, and they conducted a small logging operation, …at the outlet of Jordan Pond."[1]

So begins David Woodside's *The Story of Jordan Pond*, the restaurant that rests in the heart of America's national treasure in the northeast, Acadia National Park. Located along the beautiful coast of Maine on Mount Desert Island, it features more than its signature tea and popovers. The Pond House stands today as a world-class gathering place with a valuable heritage reaching across seven generations. But the Jordan brothers did not start a teahouse. They had a different purpose, a different vision in 1839.

The original pond house and restaurant was destroyed by fire, June 21, 1979. A brick fireplace and chimney are the only remaining vestiges. Much of the pre-restaurant era of that old house lies buried in the coffers of history and the soils along the edge of Jordan Pond. Nineteenth-century stories of Mount Desert Island offer some clues. Family genealogies, local cemeteries, and a dig into records began to reveal the story of the Jordan family from Mount Desert. This book weaves the strands of forgotten history into a memorable tapestry of adventure, heartbreak, and enduring family ties rooted there.

In 1925, George Dorr, first superintendent of Acadia, notes his intent while preserving land as a national park in a letter to Mrs. Pine, generous co-donor of additional acreage:

"... the story of its ownership should be embodied with it, for the interest of those to whom it will give pleasure in the future, to share of others which has brought that pleasure to them."[2]

---

[1] David B. Woodside, *The Story of Jordan Pond* (Bar Harbor, ME.: Acadia Corporation, 1996), 5.

[2] George B. Dorr, "Notes on Acquisition of Land," *Resource Management Records* (National Park Service, Department of the Interior: Acadia National Park, 1925), Box 1.

The discoveries which follow are also shared "for the interest of those to whom it will give pleasure" to learn. It's a story of life that echoes for me and others from the shores of Jordan Pond. As I stand along its edge, I think about the challenges faced by the family who first lived here. It adds an element of transcendence to the panoramic beauty all around me. That same beauty has enthralled generations in the past and continues to this day as earth's natural gifts are celebrated and preserved for future generations.

Life for this Jordan family took a decidedly different path than anticipated when they lived along the foot of the lake. Yet while there, they felt its richness. For the contemporary visitor, learning the story of the family that lived there might provide a new dimension to the solace of Jordan Pond.

— I —

HOW THE STORY CAME TO BE

A story of local family relatives catapulted from the back of my mind to front and center during my first term with the National Park Service in Acadia National Park.

ONE BYGONE ERA

By the time my grandmother, Myra Jordan, was growing up in the early 1900s, the eastern half of the island had changed dramatically. Her hamlet of Seal Harbor went from quaint fishing village to bustling resort with two hotels and a steamboat landing. Years later, my mother Carolyn, as a youngster, would venture back to the island with her mother to visit relatives still living in Seal Harbor in the 1930s and '40s. She never heard harrowing tales of near-missed logging disasters or how Wabanaki hunters and New England fishermen shared in the gathering of wood in the winter, wood for building as well as for burning.

Instead, Carolyn heard about all the goings-on at the Rockefeller summer residence, "The Eyrie," just up the hill, as well as the tales surrounding those from Harvard or Yale who also took up summers on the Island. How her Uncle Everett oversaw all the plumbing needs of the Rockefellers from his modest shop on Main Street. That Aunt Lena was Seal Harbor's telephone operator and the organist for the Congregational Church in the village. She also did laundry and pressed linens for wealthy notables in the area.

Carolyn overheard the stories when her mother and her Aunt Lena would get to talking. Stories about how, as the summer season ended, all the dignitaries and their families went back to their residences in New York, Philadelphia, and Boston. Auntie Lena would recount the fun that would be had over those final days before the "cottages" were winterized. (You can read elsewhere about how these residences were anything but cottages.) Like the times the help would conclude their summer duties with a mock gala. They would dress up fancy-like, saunter into the mansion's main hall, and be introduced as couples or "available." An emcee would announce "the honorable Mr. and Mrs. Watson" in an overly dignified manner. A white-gloved applause softly echoed as they bowed elegantly. Someone mimicked the dilettantes' voices, idiosyncrasies, and expressions, expounding on the latest national crisis. Howls and cackles erupted when someone would nail the expression as nearly identical to the personage. While "the guests" finished off the last of the choice food, beverages, and desserts in a "fashionable" banquet, soft ivory staccatos from the grand piano wafted throughout the hall in perfect counterpoint.

The maid proved to be a virtuoso. The help sang and danced the evening away. As hours ticked by, the water pipes were then drained and the furniture draped with dust covers. With shutters finally secured and doors bolted behind them, the caretakers surreptitiously stepped out into a frosty shimmer of the harvest moon.

Stories of that era abound. But what about further back in time, where those Jordan forebearers were involved? Why, for example, was the lake named for the Jordans and the house known as it is and not for those who catered to the wealthy all those years ago? In my early years, relatives would talk about my great-grandfather as he grew up on Jordan Pond. Visiting there as a child, then as a teen, what enamored me had little to do with history and more to do with the items on the candy or souvenir aisle.

That was before the fire of 1979. The terrible day is etched in the collective family memory, and in the memory of the locals as well. Made of century-old birchbark and spruce, the dwelling lit up like desert tinder. It rapidly reduced to ashes on that hot day in June.

The next morning, my mother and father watched as firefighters carefully navigated the rubble, looking for clues as to the fire's cause. When they discovered that my mother was a relative, one fireman retrieved a small teapot from the site. He wiped the caked soot from its green ceramic belly and presented it to her. It was a sad time for the town and the few relatives who remained. Days upon days, families on the island went about in a somber mood, as if a dear old friend had suddenly gone to Glory. An inquiry into the family of origin still had not caught my attention. That changed after thirty-plus years of maturity, when I rolled into the summer of 2014.

NAGGING QUESTIONS

I served as a Teacher Ranger at Acadia National Park, accompanying park rangers from the various divisions, learning their craft for educational purposes. The behind-the-scenes look into Acadia included perusing the wayside markers at the Jordan Pond House. On them were quotes similar to the above reference to the Jordan brothers and their logging operation. A visit to the archives at park headquarters followed. That got me in touch with an "interesting-to-know" chain of titles to the land surrounding the lake. It included my great-great-grandfather. It went back all the way to a land grant from the King of France, Louis XIV.

Then came the weekly lecture. That week's topic highlighted Acadia's history. Seated in the resource trailer at headquarters, we heard about the growing interest in land preservation by those who, having arrived on Mount Desert Island in the mid-1800s, perceived its value as a unique heritage. This led to the establishment of "Sieur de Monts National Monument," now Acadia National Park. The lecturer declared, "George Dorr was enthusiastically posting land for preservation, sometimes only minutes before the loggers arrived to claim the timber." Immediately, I sat up in my seat. *"Wait! What?"*

I lost track of the speech. My mind rocketed in another direction: *wait a minute ... my relatives ran a logging operation at Jordan Pond.* My heart rate accelerated as I got a sense of who the conflict might include. *Great-great-grampie George! Was it **his** crew being halted by the Dorr initiative?* I riveted myself to this opposing viewpoint. *Two sides to a coin,* I silently retorted. *Were my relatives the antagonists to George Dorr's "noble" land acquisition?* I adjusted my seat, trying not to appear conspicuous in my fidgeting. I cynically chuckled under my breath as the irony played out in my mind: *George Newbegin Jordan, a woodsman, the bane of the aristocrat, has a lake and a signature restaurant named after him in the middle of a park emulating the works of the wealthy!*

My thoughts took a darker turn. *But what if he actually was a victim of a land-grabbing enterprise? Was the establishment of public access done at the expense of my relatives' family business and ultimately their property?* Now this was more than just a quaint story; this involved family, relatives that my mother memorialized in our childhood trips to the island, kept resolutely in her heart as one keeps a precious locket around the neck. I had to find out more.

Living among and befriending those whose generations go back to the very first European settlements on the island has been rewarding. I have spoken with Passamaquoddy acquaintances and friends who have worked with Native American families in Maine. From these English, Irish, French Canadian, and First Nation sources, I have gained at least a cursory understanding of their sense of place and how it has changed over the years. The Jordan's sense of place holds triumph and tragedy, love and loss, disappointment and resurgence. It reflects the struggles of the region's inhabitants. It also truly embodies the Jordan family coat of arms.

WHO WERE THE JORDANS?

Percussa Resurgo – *"Struck down, I arise."*

The image of the coat comes from the middle ages. The English progenitor, Sir William Deardon…

> *an English knight, crusader in the 12th Century who, when observed by King Richard the Lion-Hearted to best a Saracen in battle after being knocked off his horse, was dubbed by the king, "Sir Jordan," after the Jordan River. Sir William subsequently requested it as a permanent name for himself, his descendants, and his home in England.*[3]

Following the Crusades, he returned to England and settled in Dorsetshire. Therein lies the origin of the "Jordain" or Jordan family.

Generations later, inhabitants of the Isles of Shoals fishing villages (a colony of Maine) wanted someone to baptize their infants and perform other duties of the clergy. The Reverend Robert Jordan had previously sailed from Dorsetshire to America in 1638 to the town of Pejepscot (Brunswick) to live with a relative who

---

[3] "Family Jordan Coat of Arms," The Family Jordan, accessed April 22, 2015, http://www.familyjordan.com/the-family-jordan-coat-of-arms/.

established the town. He was installed as the Anglican priest to Richmond Island in 1640. Marrying in 1643, he lived on the mainland with his family.

When conflicts arose with or among the area's indigenous clans, the villagers would retreat to this island across the channel (from today's Cape Elizabeth, South of Portland). As tensions subsided, they'd go back to the village. Robert's services soon extended across the channel to the mainland.

Robert's great-great-grandson Nathaniel was born in Biddeford, Maine, in 1766. He continued the impulse of the extended family's migration. He moved up the coast to Beechland along the eastern shores of Union Bay (between Ellsworth and Trenton) with his infant son, not long after his wife passed away. He occupied a farm near where his relatives Eben and Solomon Jordan farmed, and not far from where another relative, Bither Jordan, homesteaded. Nathaniel eventually married Betsy Hardin, in 1791. Together they raised fifteen children.

The farm was located near the end of what is now Beechland road. The Frenchman's Bay Conservancy has acquired Jordan family land near there and developed the old pathways as a scenic trail.

Slightly northward, the town of Ellsworth would soon emerge amidst the region's burgeoning logging industry. The children grew up and pursued various occupations, married, and raised families. Some moved from the region following gainful employment in forestry, horticulture, and architecture. Some, like George and John, stuck around.

— II —

GEORGE, JOHN, AND A FRESH START

George Newbegin Jordan teamed up with his younger brother John for a business venture in 1839.

A FAMILY BUSINESS TAKES SHAPE

In 1839, George and John Jordan's plans would come to fruition on the big island lying just south of their homestead, the one Samuel Champlain coined in 1604, *l'Ile des Monts-deserts*; Mount Desert Island. It might have been sooner had tragedy not forced priorities elsewhere. A few years before this his wife, Abigail, was taken ill after the birth of their second child, Abbie. She succumbed within three months, dying the evening before the summer solstice, 1831.

Perhaps as a friend of his sisters, Lydia Trufy came into George's life about this time. The children were growing and in need of a mother. His sisters did the best they could while he developed plans with John and worked at the blacksmith shop in town. The pain of losing Abigail was gently subsiding. Lydia was part of that healing. The two of them were married within the next year. She would help care for his young children and enable him to pursue this new enterprise with his brother.

They mortgaged nearly 3,000 acres of land in the southeastern quadrant of the island by 1839. This parcel had a curious history. The man they bought it from had recently cleared a road to the pond (now the Jordan Pond Road) and had two mills built along the creek now known as Jordan Stream. It is unclear whether the mills existed as a double mill within a single framed barn or were two separately housed sawmills situated at different points along Jordan Stream. Why the previous owner invested all that capital, building a road and two mills only to sell it off within three years of completion is unknown. It may simply have been that he set out to join in the logging boon, but a family crisis or tragedy prohibited him from pursuing his plans, not an uncommon consequence. The Jordan brothers had the skill and the drive to succeed, even though the place seemed quite obscure for a logging business. It was inland and uphill from Seal Harbor. Most sawmills were perched close to a river's shoreline or at the mouth of a bay. That way the products could be easily transported to market. Not these; it was a good two miles from the lake's nearest shoreline to the harbor. Surprisingly, the lake doesn't even appear on earlier maps of the area. When maps did chart the pond, it is shown as "Jordan's Pond."

JORDAN POND

Jordan Pond is actually classified as a lake. (The difference between a pond and a lake in the modern sense of the words has to do with the depth of vegetation. Earlier definitions of the word 'pond' had to do with a Massachusetts legislation known as "The Great Ponds Act.") The 186-acre lake is approximately 1.2 miles long North to South, and just under a half mile wide at its widest point. With an average depth of 84 feet and a maximum of 150 feet, it is the deepest lake on the island. It is also one of the clearest lakes in Maine. Typically, the lake stays clear to a depth of over 45 feet, and once in a while down to 60 feet.[1] Encompassing the current-day three-mile perimeter, a walking trail hosts a variety of scenes. Fishing is still allowed with a valid Maine fishing license. The lake's fresh water provides the locale with drinking water; thus, no large, motorized boats are permitted.

Deer Brook and another spring-fed stream that runs down the slopes of Sargent Mountain flow into it from the north. At 273 feet above sea level, the lake feeds Jordan stream which flows south into Little Long Pond, then to the ocean, at the cove called "Bracy Cove."

---

[1] "Jordan Pond," Wikipedia (Wikimedia Foundation, September 22, 2016) https://en.wikipedia.org/w/index.php?title=Jordan_Pond.

INDIGENOUS NAME
OF JORDAN POND

This land and its pond were certainly well known by First Nation inhabitants. They called the lake *mimuwipon*; that is, by what it looked like: "waters perfectly calm and smooth."[1] After paddling up what's known as Duck Brook to Eagle Lake, then portaging along a trail east of the South Bubble (now called the Jordan Pond Carry), birchbark canoes were put in, gear stowed, and swift as their maple-hewn paddles would take them, the men would cross the still waters, breech the mouth of the stream, and make their way to Little Long Pond and out to the ocean. Their true mission of seal hunting would then begin in earnest.

[1] George Neptune, "Naming the Dawnland: Wabanaki Place Names on Mount Desert Island," Mount Desert Island Historical Society, accessed December 5, 2019, https://mdihistory. org/wp-content/uploads/G. NeptuneLayout.pdf, 100.

Crossing the still waters of Mimuwipon. Sketch by RP Kline

The lumber business was booming in the early 1800s in central and northern Maine. Logs were floated down the major rivers from the north – the Penobscot, the Kennebec, and the Androscoggin. Mills were found all along the lower regions of these rivers. George and John learned about the industry along the mouth of the Union River where Ellsworth was growing.[4]

The operations, skills, and necessary equipment were all available to be apprenticed. By the time they were ready to go into business for themselves, George and John knew what went into logging and milling. What George and John had learned on the mainland, they revised to work along the rock-infested hills around the pond.

[4] Frank Greely Jordan, The Jordan Family Historical Sketches (Minneapolis, MN, 1927), 45.

The Jordans' move from the Beechland farm to the camp in Seal Harbor was harsh, yes, but there were good times too. One look at a loon's quiet approach on the still, smooth waters of the pond, one gaze at a garnet twilight behind the twin Bubble Mountains, and a deep inhale of fresh air took away the stress of a busy day. As sure as summer days were long, when chores were complete, the men and eventually their children made good use of the pond, game trails, and woods. Nowadays, swimming is prohibited. Back then it was only the chill of the water or Mother's scowl prohibiting a child's splash and a backstroke. Friends from town would show up with their fishing poles. They could commandeer a small boat to paddle over the quiet waters to their heart's content. In winter, as long as they stayed away from where the loggers worked, ice skating and ice fishing were decent occupations for the youngsters.

In between logging ventures, ice could have been harvested off the lake as it was on other ponds in the area. Alden, George's eldest child, saw ice harvesting happen on the Hadlock ponds near Northeast Harbor. He may have asked about taking ice from Jordan Pond, but it's not clear that anyone did during this era.

George's grandson, Eddie Jordan regularly took ice from Jordan Pond in the 1930s as his winter business. He maintained four "ice houses," one along the pond's shoreline, another downstream and two, closer to the village of Seal Harbor. Walking the Seaside trail from the Jordan Pond House today, there are remnants of what looks to be a foundation. Stones carefully placed in and around a rectangular space hollowed out several feet deep gives the impression this was a possible location of a storehouse for ice.

THE PROPERTY AND THE CAMP

The property George and John secured initially consisted of 2,960 acres. From the south it started at a line just above the tip of Little Long Pond. Proceeding northward up and around the lake, the acreage included two hills called the Bubbles. The western boundary included the ridges proceeding northward from Little Long Pond, up the eastern slopes and knobs of Jordan's Mountain (Penobscot Mountain). It included some of Sargent Mountain's southeastern slope. The eastern border bisected Bubble Pond and Pemetic Mountain.

Hills dominate the landscape. Their eyes automatically shifted upward to scale the height of each tree-lined ridge. Immediately, the view of that summit advanced into the next ridge and rock-lined peak, completely encircling the entire horizon. The only break in the skyline came at the mouth of Jordan Stream where a small portion of the lake's shoreline gently sloped upward through a blueberry patch. From there the gradual rise came to an opening where the house would eventually find its foundation. The valley cast southward from that point down and away toward the seashore and the village of Seal Harbor. But even there, ridges stretched like fingers along the valley, keeping another brook (Stanley Brook) from merging with Jordan Stream, all the way to the oceanfront.

And just like Maine's interior, the understory hosted everything from small cobblestones and jagged-edged boulders to fractured granite blocks. These blocks looked like they were hewn to be set as cornerstones for a life-sized Paul Bunyan Museum. Not to mention rocks known as "glacial erratics." These giant rounded hunks of volcanic rock were tumbled along and randomly situated by ancient glaciers in a most conspicuous manner.

South Bubble Mountain sports a popular glacial erratic that appears it is about to slide off the hillside and crash onto the present roadway below. (Bubble Rock) How many throngs of native Americans, French Canadian and English lumberjacks gathered to try and shove that leaning mass of granite over the edge? I'm sure the Jordan youngsters with their neighboring friends tried their luck as well.

Local histories and guidebooks, even dignitaries, acknowledged how remarkably striking the scenery and the pond itself is and makes for a beautiful setting.

"A few rods northward and we come out on Jordan's Pond, the love-liest of all the Mount Desert lakes, and one of the fairest jewels of our dear New England landscape."[5]

Historian George Street described the situation of their business as "a camp"—slightly less appealing. They certainly were not lumber barons. The house would

---

[5] M.F. Sweetser, *Chisolm's Mount Desert Guidebook* (Portland, ME: Hugh J. Chisholm, Chisolm Brothers, 1888), 60-61.

not be built for another few years. George and John occupied the "camp" to run the mills and begin work in the woods. By 1840 their business was fully underway, having completed the transfer of ownership the previous year.

Early lumber camps were rustic; one door, an opposing window, and a repugnant odor. Sketch by RP Kline

Later on, they bought a "shore lot" consisting of property starting at the low-water mark along Bracy Cove, Seal Harbor. It made up the flat land around to the east and north of Little Long Pond, including where Jordan Stream enters it up to and meeting their original property line. This would enable the brothers to cart their milled lumber down to the water's edge where it could be shipped out.[6]

It is difficult to picture nowadays, with its "carriage roads"—sculpted pathways and bridges crisscrossing the area. But if anyone meanders from the Pond House to the water's edge and looks over to the left, there's a spillway and a small bridge. Standing at that bridge's vantage point, a visitor would be directly within the heart of the Jordan operations, back in 1840.

---

[6] It is not clear that the "shore lot" mentioned in the probate records is on Bracy Cove. It could have been along the western side of Seal Harbor. But assuming descriptions matching the field and lane along Little Long Pond are accurate, I chose to assign this lot at Bracy Cove. Hancock County Probate Office, GN Jordan file,1863.

This was an exciting time, but a challenging one. The family was apart. Initially, Lydia, Alden, and Abbie—George's wife and two children—lived back on the mainland while the brothers "commuted" to the lakefront. A wooden bridge connecting the island had opened three years earlier. Captain William Thompson and John M. Noyes contracted for the bridge to be built during the winter of 1836-37, the winter before the brothers found out about the property going up for sale.

When the land was theirs, they got some horses, hitched up the wagons, loaded them with supplies, gear, and belongings, and set off for Thompson's Bridge. They continued down the trail to Somes Sound. There they boarded their supply wagons on a large raft or barge, horses and all. The brothers would sail around to Seal Harbor then trudge the supplies to the camp. Going to work was anything but easy.

GETTING UNDERWAY

The brothers worked together, performing multiple tasks. Unless time or volume required otherwise, they ran the whole operation as a partnership until Alden was old enough to help. George had the primary task of mill operations. If their total wood volume was small, they would work the woods first, felling timber. Then later, haul it to the mill. But if it was a larger enterprise, or the mill had to run during times when wood cutting was in progress, then John took on the lumbering responsibilities, hiring other loggers to pitch in.

Standing alongside Jordan Pond it is hard to imagine anything but contemplation happening there. Poetry, pigments of watercolor and oils, songwriting; fishing, maybe. But logging? By the time the Pond House became a place for tea and popovers, much of the old growth forest had been supplanted. George and John did much of that harvesting.

LIFE IN THE WOODS

A woodsman's work along the lakeshore in one sense was exactly what it was in any forest anywhere. Work in the woods involved two stages: chopping and hauling. Chopping down the trees ideally happened at the height of winter when the hardwood was the lightest and sap slows to a crawl in conifers. Hauling continued for the rest of the season.

A team of woodsmen would gather at a stand of trees to clear-cut. Each man had at least an axe. Some carried a two-person broad-toothed saw. This common saw, called a "whipsaw," had handles on both ends for cutting the tree or downed trunk with another person.

Later in the 1800s, this type of saw could actually be used solo if necessary. There was such a thing called a "rubber man."[7] The sawyer took along a heavy-duty strip of rubber. He would drive an iron rod into the ground and attach one end of the rubber securely to the rod. The other end would be tied to the whipsaw's opposing handle. The woodsman would then move around to the other side of the tree trunk, position the saw, his side being closest to the tree. As he pulled back, the rubber strap would stretch, supplying the necessary resistance to "pull" the saw back into position after the first bite. The sawyer would go ahead like that, albeit much slower than with an actual partner. This would make a fellow mighty hungry, but it served as an effective replacement for the lacking help in the long run.

The Rubber Man allowed a lumberjack to manage without a partner, but barely. Sketch by RP Kline.

---

[7] This tactic is not well documented in its use in the Maine woods. The vulcanization of rubber and development of such bands was just appearing in 1840.

Food was often "toted" to the logging site on a dogsled made for the job. This labor-intense task often fell to a younger person known as "the cookee." Sometimes, a meal would be toted right up to where the lumbermen were working. A huge pot of pork and beans, strong tea, and some biscuits or hardtack would be delivered. If the load didn't tip off the sled before arrival, the men would enjoy a short break to down the victuals and warm their innards. They would not sit long since the day was cold, and the work was plenty. Rarely a grumble was heard, though, when the tote sled arrived with food.

Eventually, after the family joined him at the camp, George's children vied for the task of sledding the tote up to the work crew. It got them out of the camp and away from Lydia's watchful eye. She made sure her hard work of cooking that meal was packed safely on the sled. Alden enjoyed the job most of the time. He was older though not necessarily wiser than his sister, Abbie, in those formative days of the camp's operations.

If there was any advantage to winter harvesting it was found in the area's snowpack. At a depth of three to eight feet of densely compacted snow, woodsmen could traverse the hills in snowshoes and set down a useful trail for packing-in supplies. That trail might well serve for hauling out logs—either by horse and flank-rope, a snub-line, or oxen with log sleds. Amidst this foreboding landscape which most lumberjacks avoided for its danger and difficulty stood the dense coniferous forest of white pine, balsam fir, spruce, cedar, and hemlock. There were also hardwood areas of grey birch, oak, and maple, all ripe for harvest. A beautiful sight for tourist and forester alike. Streams popping out of the hillsides flowing downward created breaks in the rock-filled, snowcapped understory. The artist's canvas could take advantage of the scenery. But few lumbermen relished the thought of harvesting timber there along the slopes.

LOGGING PRACTICES

During this era little thought was given to forest replenishment. The sparse human population, the vast stretches of virgin timber, even on the island, provided little if any notion that the supply might not outlast the demand. Reforestation, the concern for forest habitat, or the highly valuable forest management practices of today simply did not enter into their thinking. It wasn't until late in the Jordan brothers' experience that the scarcity of island forests even began to arise in the newly arriving public's consciousness.

http://www.greatnorthwoods.org/logging/cliftonjohnson/2.htm

John and George wisely set to work on the lower hills first, nearest Seal Harbor. Getting used to the equipment, animals, and terrain, they would work northward. They began at the lower elevations, clearing the way for timber higher up. Gradually, the woodsmen chopped their way upward, ascending the steep edges of the lakeshore's hills.

There were techniques that helped the common woodsman to complete his work with success and kept him alive. There were methods that, if they failed, could cost the lives of everyone and every animal involved. Nevertheless, a day in the woods was always filled with hard work, often with teamwork, and at the end a sense of satisfaction.

The hauling endeavor required creative adjustments from what occurred in the upland portions of Maine. The foreman, whether George or John, arranged for any heavier equipment needed for the terrain to move the timber from the felling place to a gathering location, or in most instances, directly down to awaiting teamsters or boom operators—those managing logs on the lake's open waters. Log sleds, flank ropes for horses, pulleys, or the ropes making up a "snub-line" were used for getting large logs down a slope without killing the animals or the woodsmen.

Horses were more agile on the rocky hills than were oxen. But horses were in short supply for the Jordans. Although oxen were readily available, they were limited to more level terrain. When they worked near the pond, lumbermen could create a path in which large logs could slide down the sides of the hills and onto the ice or into the water. Logs would often sustain damage using this process. So it's likely the Jordans put the snub-line method to good use. Once down the slopes, logs could then be carted by the oxen or guided toward the outlet and the mill.

That snub-line apparatus bears the notorious reputation of being the deadliest of all the contraptions a woodsman would encounter in the entire Maine woods. A teamster brought his team and sled to the top of the slope. Logs were loaded onto the sled. He took a "hawser," a very thick rope, and attached it around and to the back of the sled. It was secured at the back of the rig with half-hitches that would tighten as later, the heavy load settled onto the rope. Logs were then chained tightly atop the sled. On up the slope a ways, the hawser had been wrapped several times around a four-foot stump of the largest tree at the upper edge of the clear-cut. The rope was long, about double the trip down the hill. The teamster climbed up on the top of the load, then when ready, clucked to the horses. The teamster dished out the rope slowly as it wound around the stump and the team moved cautiously down the hill. He steadied himself, holding the end of the hawser, watching the stump like a hawk. If it all worked correctly, the team and the load would arrive at the base of the hill and, on level ground, the driver would release the rope and be done with the snub-line.

The Snub-line was dangerous to man and animal alike. Sketch by RP Kline.

The Jordan brothers probably adapted this snub-line strategy to work on single logs without the horses or smaller loads as well. Lines would be well used by the Jordans. Whether by a sled team or for single or small tightly wrapped free-standing log loads, ropes were a critical part of their inventory. There were a lot of slopes to cover. If a rope was worn, its shiny surface was a tell-tale sign it should be replaced. If only one tiny strand of the rope caught on a sharp spot of that stump up the hill, with the weight of the load of logs on the sled, that taut rope would fray, then unwind like a spring and snap. The jolt would be immediately felt by the driver, sitting on top of the load. He would crack his whip and let the horses try and outrun the load now careening downhill behind them. It was a race with death that, if won, would be the stuff of legend.

Once down on level ground, teamsters preferred areas where ice was thick so the sled topped with tons of timber could slide easily. The Jordans duplicated this process. Across the pond or down a frozen path, the Jordans used their own oxen or borrowed horses for transport. At Jordan Pond, the distance across the lake was relatively short. Logs could be skidded across the ice to a gathering place along the southwest shore. The beasts of burden, if they had to haul across ice, wore shoes with spikes called "calks" to remain stable.

If confined to tote roads and pathways, the ideal setting was found in late winter or early March as the snow melted in the daytime and froze solid on the paths overnight. The lumbermen loaded up a sled in the late afternoon to prepare for an early morning trek over the smooth ice.

Hauling would go on in this fashion as long as there was snow and ice to move upon. If hauling extended past the time of the thaw or happened in the fall before the lake froze over, loggers had their own unique method of traversing open lake water. The logs were gathered in a "boom," a floating rope cast around the wide group of floating logs. The ends were held together with a length of rope extended to a raft holding a man-powered windlass. The raft's anchor was thrown out as far as it could go. Then the men turned the windlass and drew the load toward the anchor. This two-step process was repeated until the lake was traversed.

A dam held back the waters of the pond and supplied waterpower to the mill (located right about where the spillway is today). This was where the boomers would end their navigation. The logs were hoisted out of the water and onto an area where they were de-barked and prepared for milling. This arduous technique reminded the men why they liked to work in winter when the ice made hauling easier.

Winter was also the best time for hiring added help if it was needed. Fishing slowed on the island and, while most of the Wabanaki families would migrate back to their inland habitat, some would remain to find work in the area. Farmers would also look for additional sources of income during the winter months.

A SAWMILL AT JORDANS POND

After the land purchase in 1839, George and John furnished the existing logging camp for the work along the newly charted pond. The mill used the pond's outflow into Jordan Stream as the energy source for the common sawmill powertrain, a waterwheel-driven saw.

The mill the Jordans used[8] was likely the standard frame constructed for that time period. The millrace was formed over the natural fall of the pond through the mouth of the stream leading southward to Little Long Pond. That edge of the

---

[8] According to the description of the land purchased by the Jordan brothers, a mill with its supporting out buildings already existed on the property. Source: "Series VIII: Land Files. Land Deeds: Transferred from JD Rockefeller, Jr. *Abstract of Title of Land in Mount Desert, Near Jordans Pond, Hancock County, Maine, Deed 140.*" Box 132, Folder 6." Bar Harbor: Acadia National Park, n.d., 24.

lake formed a pool that, when dammed up, could continuously power the mill throughout the year.

Mills employing waterwheels saw upwards of 1,000 gallons per minute flow over it, so much water the wheels themselves could not be seen for the furious motion of its running. Given the layout of the pond and stream, the Jordans probably utilized an additional means of power: the underwater turbine. Of course, steam power was quickly becoming popular by 1850. They could have wrested a steam engine from an abandoned ship's anchor or sail winch system. George and John might have retrofitted the pre-existing mill with steam power. But the combination of frugality with expedience—that is, the convenience of using ample waterpower with a sturdy mill already existing—seems to favor a typical waterwheel-turbine-powered sawmill.

Mill operations harnessed basic physics, cascading linkages of power from the waterwheel to a reciprocating saw. This eight-to-ten-foot blade is held in place by an apparatus called a gang sash that allows the up-down cutting motion to be held secure. Saw power comes through a series of drive belts, cams, ratchets, and shafts with "wobbler joints."

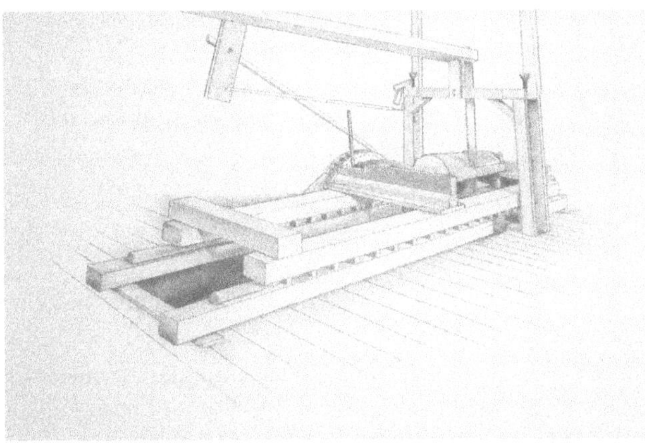

The reciprocating saw powered by a waterwheel became the standard by the time Maine became a state. Sketch by RP Kline.

Logs would be "debarked," that is, their bark removed, then rolled in on an incline and hoisted to rest on a carriage in line with the saw unit. The carriage was underlain with protruding "teeth" which meshed with a crankshaft. Hooked to an escape wheel, the ratchet gear prohibited reverse motion, a similar function to that of a clock spring. With the engagement of the clutch, this set to cranking the carriage forward toward the moving saw blade and sash unit. When the log's beam was cut, a turbine resting in the streambed underneath the carriage was engaged to shoot the carriage back into its original place. The log, then repositioned, was set for the next cut. This carried on until the entire log had been processed. The lumber would be moved to a place to cure or dry out. Stacks were often sheltered from the elements by lean-tos, open pavilion-like sheds, or in regular barns where heat could build up and dry out all types of wood in all its shapes.

Many tasks were at once the work of only a few people, save in the larger mills. There was the sawyer, who controlled the saw and the movement of the log along the carriage rail. This person was supported by the ratchet-setter, who was as quick-minded and nimble as the sawyer. They worked as a highly synchronized team. An off-bearer managed all of the waste products from the cut. He kept the leftover bark, wane, and debris away from the sash and saw unit. The log-roller—perhaps two people—set the log in place after each cut using peaveys or look-hooks, a mill version of the river driver's "can't dog."

There were millwrights, sophisticated troubleshooters. These men knew the mill's every square inch—every shaft, gear, pulley, wheel, and how they operated—since they were tasked with repairing any malfunction. They also had to sharpen the saw blades by hand. They would grind to specs each tooth of that reciprocating saw with a file. Laborious, yes; due not so much to the number of teeth in the saw, but due to the angle of the teeth on a vertical saw. During the off season, blades could be removed, then sharpened on a workbench. After hours, when the sluiceway was closed and the waterwheel quiet, even if another blade was available, sharpening the saw blade in place on the sash was expedient during the busy season.

As cited below, at smaller, family-run mills, all these tasks were done by one, maybe two, people, and by hand. George, his young teenage son Alden, and John were the ones who handled the bulk of operations at Jordan Pond. When, as a young adult, Alden married and moved to Massachusetts, he was known as a "millman." He had learned to perform each and every task under his father's tutelage. Alden later returned to work with his father and uncle at a key point in the mill's operation.

Records show on average a healthy flow of lumber came from small, family-run mills:[1]

- Some water-powered mills produced over 250,000 board feet of lumber per year (an average of 700 board feet per day) by the mid-1830s.

- Small, family-owned mills which employed from six to eight laborers produced about 300,000 to 450,000 board feet of lumber per year (about 1,300 board feet per day).

- These small mills were run by the owner and his family, with seasonal help being hired during peak production periods.

These mills mainly served the local area.

---

[1] Gary Katz, et al, "Hull-Oakes Sawmill," THIS is Carpentry, Accessed 3/19/2016, https://www.thisiscarpentry.com/2011/02/25/hull-oakes-sawmill/.

The Jordan brothers constructed other buildings surrounding the mill which resourced the operation. The farmhouse that became famous would eventually lie uphill where George's family, then later on John's family, shared life together. For now, a barn, a blacksmithing shop, and a carriage house all sat within easy access. Planks, posts and boards, shingles, shakes and stakes came out of the mill. Initially stacked to dry, the materials were loaded onto oxcarts and horse-drawn wagons or sleds and carried to Seal Harbor or the Bracy Cove shoreline. There the Jordans would get a fair price from buyers near the island's south coast.

Customers could be found at Seal Harbor, Northeast Harbor, along Somes Sound, and the smaller isles just offshore. The fishery, by that time, found in Bass Harbor, may have had repair needs if the mills there ran low. A call might have come from those new construction operations in the Bar Harbor area. They might have even gotten word from a relative in the Ellsworth ship-building industry, although it would have been a long haul over land or water, or both.

Those Jordan relatives built a schooner in 1863, later named *General Meade,* following the battle at Gettysburg.

Richard Walden Hale, *The Story of Bar Harbor, an Informal History Recording One Hundred and Fifty Years in the Life of a Community* (New York: I. Washburn, 1949), 124.

Other machines were at work around the mill. Turbine-clutch systems ran planers, shingle makers, and lathes. With all those operations accompanying the feverish tempest of the mill's primary function, this was a noisy but, more seriously, a hazardous place. Tales and ballads written during that era lament the loss of life and limb. Accidents, both in the mill and the woods that supported them, reveal that Mainers and migrants who worked there bore a lion's share of suffering.

Milling timber creates another interesting phenomenon: a steadily growing mound of sawdust. Some of them grew to magnanimous proportions. Once the mill quieted for the evening or a Sabbath rest, aromatic sawdust hills provided the children with hours of fort-digging and sledding. Sawdust from this mill likely piled up downstream amongst the eddies of the twists and turns of Jordan Stream.

Some sawdust piles along lakesides have remained in existence for more than a century. One can be seen today along the shore of Ambajejus Lake, near Millinocket, Maine. They turn into homes for cliff swallows and objects of curiosity for kayakers.

FAMILY LIFE

During this time, John had been courting Lucy Hardin, a distant relative of his mother. He had been bunking at the camp with his brother from the outset. But deciding that Lucy would make a much better roommate than George, John married her in August 1839. They found a more suitable place for newlyweds to live in Northeast Harbor, about three miles away. That left the camp open for George's young family to eventually join him there. Alden was ten, Abbie, eight years old. Lydia occupied her time with the children, then eventually organized the camp for operations at the mill.

The pond, forests, and clearing supplied much of their needed sustenance. Lydia and the children were able to create a bearable life, with a little ingenuity and a lot of hard work. During that era women ran the homestead, as it were, especially in winter as the men were occupied with lumbering.

Lydia bartered with families nearby to gather necessities. She and the children oversaw the livestock, poultry, and their garden's produce. Preserving as much as they could helped them get through the harsh winter. Luckily, the pond did have some fish that a hole in the ice and a pole might provide if meat was sparse. Alden and Abbie got to be rather good at fishing. George was a blacksmith as well as a lumberman. Folks from town would bring him equipment needing repair or ask him to make a special implement for their team of oxen or horses. He could trade the work for use of the team come log-hauling time.

Lydia was usually vibrant and healthy. While the operation of the mill at the camp had continued since its purchase in 1839, she had been in charge of the children, then life at the camp. George's first wife, Abigail, had lost her battle with infection not long after their second child was born. Lydia had stepped in within a year and, while they had no children together, she spent eleven years by George's side, raising Alden and Abbie and keeping things going. From the Beechland farmstead to the camp at the pond, Lydia was there every step of the way. She was looking forward to the house George and John were building. Plans were made. Lumber was set aside as much as they could afford. And by 1844, Lydia could almost see the effort starting to come together up on the knoll above the camp. But living in a rustic logging camp was not an ideal situation—a step down from the Beechland farm. By the time 1845 rolled around, an ailment had overtaken her strength. The cemetery shows that Lydia was buried in July of that year.

The logging camp was a grungy, unforgiving domicile where unsupervised youngsters might be in harm's way. George had responsibilities for the work. John would do what he could but had a family of his own to care for. George's mother lived with one of his sisters on the mainland. There might be some possibility of the sisters taking on the challenge of the youngsters. The circumstances and severity of life made it clear George needed to find a partner. Someone to care for the children and look after the camp and eventually the home. George married a gal named Hannah Stephens from the Cranberry Isles before the next winter.

It is still a mystery how this relationship evolved. They may have known each other's families. A suggestion may have arisen through John or his wife's acquaintances. Hannah might even have been a nurse for Lydia during her illness. Young women were being hired on the island for a host of duties, especially as newcomers were beginning to show up. A caregiver in the camp certainly would prove beneficial. How it ever came to be, by late 1846 George and Hannah had become husband and wife and the house up on the hill continued to its completion. Alden, seventeen, and Abbie, fifteen, were now under the care of twenty-two-year-old Hannah Stephens Jordan.

Was she ready to take on the responsibility of two teenagers at a new home on the pond? There were a few incentives. The house was coming along, and by the following year it would be ready to move into. It was a beautiful setting. And not far from her home on Great Cranberry Island. She had cared for younger siblings and cousins back home. Hannah was quite familiar with hardship, as were most women of the archipelago. She made a way and took on the task before her.

Moving uphill from camp to the newly constructed farmhouse was a welcome event. Along with settling in, there was subsistence farming, which had already been a mainstay at the Jordan residence. An apple orchard; a small garden of corn, peas, beans, and potatoes; a pen for the domestic animals–chickens, a cow, and perhaps sheep, a goat or pig, had long since provided routines for Abbie and Alden. By this time, the older Alden got, the more he spent time with his father in the mill. Thus, Abbie and Hannah made short work of the chores outside in order to be busy with the new house needing attention.

THE JORDANS' FARMHOUSE

Between the two, John and George had enough skill and resources to supply a well-built, timber-frame home. Crafted according to tradition, the home took shape in the English style, just like their father's and grandfather's before them.

> A similar structure is found at Acadia National Park's Carroll Homestead, near Southwest Harbor.

They staked out the building's footprint, painstakingly digging and securing stone footings, and digging the root cellar. Digging was met with resistance. The subsoil held rocks of various proportions. Partially buried boulders could be clearly seen all around the area..

The brothers framed out the house, closed it in, then began the finer carpentry of the inside walls, cabinet making, and trim. Its "mortice and tenon" construction created a secure fit at the corners that needed few, if any, nails. A brick fireplace and chimney were the centerpiece of the home. An inner section of the house featured the fireplace, its mantle, a staging area for the cooking utensils, and an oven for baking. In back of the brickwork, cabinetry housed a dry storage area, complete with shelving for storing flour, grain, and spices, and for warming bread, pies, and other goodies. Around that central section all the other rooms branched out and up. The kitchen, one bedroom, and a parlor occupied the main floor. An upstairs area sectioned off three rooms with dormer windows. No refrigeration meant a cool, drying area with meat hooks attached to the ceiling for butchered meat or curing game. The ice box cabinet filled with sawdust allowed ice harvested from either this lake or others nearby to be used almost the entire year. No plumbing meant a dry sink indoors and a privy somewhere outside.

Windows and oil lamps were abundant since it would be a long time before electricity was introduced. The central fireplace heated the house by way of open ventilation and very carefully chosen cobbles or leftover bricks. Open ventilation meant literal holes in the wall and ceiling with grates covering them. Larger cobblestones were better than bricks because they were easier on the toes when placing them for warmth under the blankets at the foot of the bed. The brothers finished the house and its interior by mid-1847.

THE VILLAGE DOWNHILL

Seal Harbor is a community not too far downhill. There were new folks coming from far away and building homes up on the hill east of the village. It was busier than in earlier times. Some of the established families likely welcomed Hannah to the neighborhood. Captain John Bracy was from a homesteader family. Having known the Jordans from when they occupied the camp, he and his wife Barbara Bracy knew of Lydia's passing. They may not only have attended the funeral but supplied George with a burial plot for Lydia. The current gravestone shows the plot is shared by the Jordan and Bracy families.

Now that Hannah was part of the Jordan family, she and Barbara would have things in common. Barbara had already been a mother for several years. She and her children knew Alden and Abbie. Barbara was preparing to give birth to her fourth child around the same time Hannah was preparing to have her first, in the summer of 1847. Barbara could possibly have been a welcome support for Hannah during this time and through the years. They would have several more children around the same time as each other. Barely a month after little George (Junior) was born in October of 1854, Barbara's son Augustus was born. The two boys grew up together and quite possibly became friends. The Bracy home along the ocean shore and the Jordan home along the Pond were filled with childhood laughter and consternation. They shared life's adventures growing up in Seal Harbor amidst the swelling influx of "rusticators"—what visitors fancied themselves as—who invaded the island in the summertime.

Watercolor by Thomas J. Reeverts.

III

TURBULENCE AND TRAGEDY

Calm before the storm: a fitting metaphor for the coming years at Jordan Pond.

GROWING UNREST

The years from 1855-1862 were turbulent across the nation and across the island. Economic downturns were severe. The Civil War was brewing, yet the island's villages were hosting more and more visitors. It wouldn't be long before bed-and-breakfast-type accommodations would soon give way to immense hotels. Eventually "cottages," mansions really, were being built across Eden (Bar Harbor), Northeast Harbor, and Southwest Harbor. Even Seal Harbor was undergoing a swell of busyness in its streets and shops. By the end of the war, Mount Desert Island had its portent of growing opulence.

Alden had married in 1850 and moved to Boston. Abbie had married and moved to Saugus, Massachusetts, within two years of that. Hannah, by 1855, had four of her own children in the house: Cedelia (1847), Melvina (1849), Alice Jane (1852), and George (1854). They kept busy with chores, occasional visits by seasonal help walking up from the mill, and passersby who came to the end of the Jordan road just to see what was there. The mill work was at its peak despite the nearby forest fire of 1852—as was often the case, a blueberry patch "prescribed burn" may have gone out of control.

In 1858 Alden returned with his wife and family, settling on Little Cranberry Island. He pitched in at the mill. It was a good thing too. George and John had their hands full keeping up with orders. Ironically, despite the boon in construction, there was a growing discontent with logging crews. The summer guests were beginning to complain that the forests were disappearing. Not seeing the connection, their call for lumber continued.

The years 1863 and 1864 would prove to be the major turning point for the Jordan family. The Civil War had caused the Union to call for volunteer soldiers from each state. Some of the boys from Seal Harbor enlisted and went to Rockland to sign up. Fewer men were available to work. Businesses slowed production. The few craftsmen who were left needed less wood products.

As if this weren't enough, illness was making its way through the island's households. George Jordan wasn't doing well. He may have been suffering with symptoms of tuberculosis or a form of cancer unknown at the time. Augustus Bracy, the childhood friend of little George (or Junior, as they may have called him), had taken sick awhile back. He hadn't been seen in days. Even as a young boy his health was deteriorating. Diphtheria was claiming the life of many a child here and on the mainland. It is not known what Augustus was struggling with, but by the end of 1863 he was buried in the shared Jordan-Bracy plot in Seal Harbor Cemetery.

ACCIDENT, DISEASE, OR BOTH?

The family story told through the generations is that George was killed in an accident in the mill. On the 9th of March,[9] he died from what his obituary called "*consumption.*" That was the term for tuberculosis (TB). It was also a general description of when the actual cause was either overly complex or difficult to diagnose. Tuberculosis could have set in without any signs, decades before they began work on the island.[10]

Twenty-five years of breathing sawdust and working along the granite outcroppings which produce small amounts of radon could exacerbate, if not approximate, the symptoms of TB. Those symptoms include severe involuntary muscle contraction or cramping. It is conceivable George may have experienced something of this sort while at work in the mill, putting him in harm's way of the saw, the moving carriage, or the like. George died just two months shy of his sixtieth birthday.

FIRE!

Fire broke out on the south end of the island. It started in the driest part of the season, 1864. Lightning perhaps. Maybe another burned blueberry patch gone rogue. The wildfire ripped through the treetops, creating its own weather. A firestorm surged down the creases into the valleys. A pale-orange outline of the hills could be seen from Seal Harbor's wharf. The white-hot wind drove over the southern slopes, heading for the village. The heat scorched everything in its path, including the soil. Jordan Pond and Upper and Lower Hadlock Ponds were the only firebreaks. The fire dissipated, though, just before rolling over the Jordan house and buildings.

---

[9] Documents conflict as to the exact date and year of death. The dates differ from March 9, 10, or 19. The year stated as 1863 or 1864.

[10] Tuberculosis," Mayo Clinic (Mayo Foundation for Medical Education and Research, April 3, 2021), https://www.mayoclinic.org/diseases-conditions/tuberculosis/symptoms-causes/syc-20351250. Accessed 4/17/2021.

Watercolor by Thomas J Reeverts.

With the autumn chill came frantic questions. What were they to do? How would the work continue without timber? No one replanted conifers or reseeded hardwood clearings during this era. Besides, it takes years to grow to a height worth harvesting. Few, if any, hardwoods survived.

THE CIVIL WAR'S ADVERSE EFFECTS

"The draft in Maine has a dubious history," wrote historian Tim Garrity. A town quota was in effect and there was a price to pay if that quota was not met. A loophole allowed some to "hire a substitute" who would go in the place of the draftee. Poorer families had seen their sons and fathers end up heading to the battlefront,[11] while those of more substantial means were able to remain at home to carry on business as usual.

In a letter from Emily to Augustus (Chase) Savage, one of the townspeople, you can just feel the anguish over the struggles that continued.

At Home March 27, 1865, Dear Chase,

Once more I seat myself to answer your kind letter of the 18th.... Oh, I am so glad you have not had to stand the draft. It has come off in our town and it has gone very hard on us …. and it has taken our best and poorest men there is. Not one able to hire a substitute except Sans. He will if he is excepted [accepted] but he thinks he won't as he is so very blind…. and there is Alden. There is three families that looks to him for help. Mr. Jordan says he can't do a thing in the

---

[11] Tim Garrity, "The War at Home: Copperheads Down East, 1861-1865," *Chebacco*, Vol. 15, 2014, 56.

mill if Alden goes to war as Alden is boss of the work. They all that are at home have gone to Belfast to be examined. I both long and dread for them to get home again for to have so many men go out of this little neighborhood twill be so very lonesome.[12]

Three families depended on Alden: his own on Little Cranberry Island, his stepmother Hannah's family (George had been gone now at least a full year), and Alden's uncle John's family, since John could not run the operations himself..

The end of the Civil War came in April 1865, so this draft never went into effect. Worrying over Alden passed. But so many in the surrounding villages were already affected. It had to have an impact on their business as well.

Besides things unraveling at the mill—the fire, the loss of his partner, the threat of the war's draft—John's wife contracted an illness. Now he had more to think about. But keeping the business alive became vital. With the war over and Alden spared from the draft, John's thought was to keep the mill running as long as possible. He needed resources to pay the doctor. Alden needed resources for those in his care. There may have been timber still standing at the head of the pond and over the saddle onto the shores of Young's Pond (Eagle Lake). But with the huge loss from last year's fire and now with his wife's increasing illness, John began to see it was nearly impossible to keep going. His two daughters, Philena and Elizabeth, could be by her side so he might tend to the work—what work there was left to supervise.

When John's wife passed in the fall of 1865, he may have had so much debt, he was worried about those who had loaned him resources to get through. His friend Captain John Bracy may have brought medicine from Boston on his recent trip. He may have offered some to John, even though most of it was meant for his own wife, Barbara. She was not well either.

---

[12] Emily Savage (Mount Desert, Maine, March 27, 1865) Mount Desert Historical Society. Accessed August 2015.

IV

DEALING WITH LOSS

The severity and hardships of life in this era affected families on many levels.

John, Alden, Hannah, and her children certainly were feeling the force of circumstance. Uncertainty and grief blurred their focus. The trouble seemed relentless. Each was struck with a loss of industry and family members.

How would the Jordan children be comforted without their father George? He is described as a kind and gentle man. Was he their cheerful distraction from winter's harshness? Would he wrestle with Junior after the two of them finished stocking firewood for the kitchen? Was he the special guest at the evening teatime with the girls? More than once, George came home from the mill mid-winter and grabbed a bundle of flour from the cellar to help out a struggling family. A deacon in Ellsworth Baptist Church, he lived out his faith. He was missed on many levels.

Now all of that was gone. How would the girls respond to the void? Cedelia, the eldest, was she quiet? Would she stick close to Mother and take her cues from the stalwart, stoic routines that kept the house from going into shambles? Within a year, at only age seventeen and a half, she would marry John Clement, son of a long-standing family in Seal Harbor. Alice Jane, age eleven, and Junior, age nine, were likely preoccupied by daily childhood worries. *I'm cold! AJ took my spoon! My knee hurts. I miss Daddy …*

MELVINA – WEDNESDAY'S CHILD

Fifteen-year-old Melvina found it difficult to adjust. Or so it seems. Was there a gnawing absence grief could not erase? After the arid months without her father's influence, she found solace in someone's arms, leaving her pregnant, unmarried, and alone to face immeasurable shame.

Families either split apart or were brought closer together by circumstances such as these. It is not clear whether Hannah ever made her feel as though she were an outcast or a failure. Certainly Melvina could supply enough of that all by herself. Every look by the townspeople could be construed as one of disdain. There probably was an awkwardness with her own sisters which felt isolating. And to make matters worse, never once did the family hear from the boy that fathered the child. Could it be that he had entered the Civil War and never returned?

The pregnancy went full term, with Melvina giving birth to a baby boy in May 1865. Melvin came into this world like any other child of that time. But it was not without complications. Melvina became increasingly ill as the days of her infirmity turned into weeks. She was too frail to nurse, even though at sixteen, she was in the prime of youth. Heartbreak hit the family again as she succumbed to infection by August 1865.

Melvin became the youngest member of the Jordan family, as was the tradition in those days. Hannah took him in as one of her own. If Melvina were a sweet middle daughter, in the end her memory would be less honorable than she deserved, perhaps. And it was to be the same for Melvin, always under suspicion for being so young compared to the other siblings.

SAYING GOODBYE TO THE POND HOUSE

Gathering again at the shared gravesite of the Jordans and Bracys, Barbara Bracy was laid to rest. Eventually, both Captain Bracy and Hannah Jordan realized how much life the families already shared. So, they were married on August 12, 1866. Many families in this era merged to survive, perhaps more than for affection. Captain John moved Hannah and her youngest, Alice Jane, George Junior, and toddler Melvin, from the pond house to his home along the cove west of Seal Harbor.

Captain Bracy's house was situated along the area near where the Harbor club now stands.

With the house along the pond now vacant, John would take this opportunity to sell his home in Northeast Harbor and move into the pond house. He would pay off some debts by continuing his work at the mill, albeit a mere skeleton of what once flourished there.

John would inhabit the place with his children and eventually his new wife for those final years. Probate court would determine how the land and resources would be divided and debts paid. The fire of '64 burned out most of their "inventory." John may have made a promise to some local merchants that he would keep the mill open a while longer, with Alden's help. There was more work that could be done, but only scant amounts remained for cutting. Others would have to bring wood to supply the mill with work.

INVOLVING THE COURTS

To the Hon. Parker Tuck, Judge of probate for Hancock County

John S Jordan, of Mount Desert in said county respectfully represents, that Geo. N. Jordan, late, of said Mount Desert, deceased, was at the time of his death tenant in common with said John S. Jordan, of an undivided tract of land situated in Eden and Mount Desert in said county, each owning one half; that at a term of the Probate Court at Ellsworth, for said county, on the second Wednesday, of April, 1873, upon the petitions of the heirs of Geo. N. Jordan, three commissioners …were appointed to make partition of said tract and to set out to John S. Jordan one half thereof, to be held by him in severalty …. all to the west of said line with mill, carriage house, one half of dwelling house, one half of barn and one half of the blacksmith shop, that in their return of said partition by said commissioners made to Probate Court, at a term held at Ellsworth for said County on the first Wednesday of September, A. D. 1875, the commissioners omitted to describe the said part set out to John S. Jordan. Wherefore John S. Jordan prays that the commissioners may amend their return by stating therein the parcel set out to John S. Jordan, and as in duty bound will ever pray.

JOHN S. JORDAN

Nov. 3, 1880[13]

Probate drags on. In this case for almost two decades after George's passing. Alden had petitioned early on to become administrator of his father's estate in February 1867. In doing so, he hoped to settle the business and family debts that arose before his father's death. As the eldest son from George's first marriage, he was granted the responsibility, after posting a $1,500 bond with the help of two friends, noting that Hannah had remarried. The estate included one-half the original land acquisition in 1839. An inventory of buildings included little more than the mill and the house as noted above. The remaining equipment included blacksmithing tools, a plow, six ox chains, and a rifle. Probate records show the sad reality which debt played against families even back then. More and more acreage was exacted by the courts to pay off debtors.

The first to be sold satisfied a one hundred-fifty-dollar debt. Then, three hundred; another, six hundred dollars. Considering the nearby burned-over land sold at one point for as low as fifty cents an acre, one wonders what large portions of the property going up for sale would bring. John, probably fearing his half of the property would be either underpriced or seized, petitioned the court to secure

---

[13]   John S Jordan, "Published Letter to Probate Court," in *Ellsworth American*, 1880.

his part as separate from the estate's holding. Alden and the other siblings likely feared the entire estate would shrivel before them. Ultimately, they would inherit a mere fraction of the total land originally purchased—less than two hundred acres. George, Jr. would later buy the pond itself from the estate, hence the name, "Jordan Pond," remained intact.

A WIDOW'S DOWER

Additionally, the court confirmed what Massachusetts law had established a century before. There was to be a portion of the land set aside to be the sole possession of the widow of the deceased. Neither Alden as estate administrator nor debtors could seize that property until the widow's passing. A court order could reduce but not eliminate the plot. This was a critical asset, a valuable possession, something to protect the widow from becoming destitute.

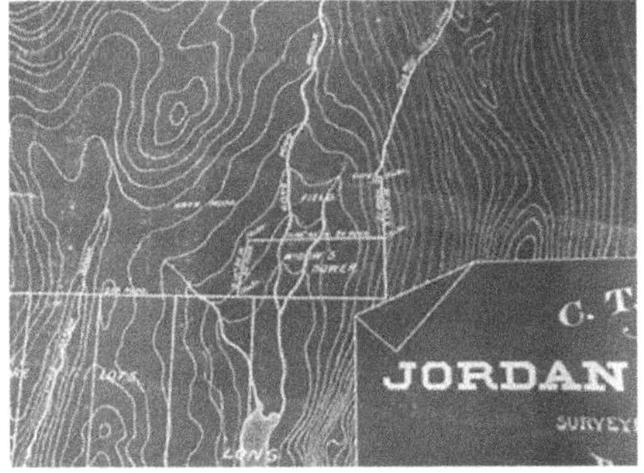

"Widow's Dower location on CT How's Jordan Pond Lot Survey Map. EM Hamper, Surveyor. Surveyed November 1882. Map Courtesy of Hancock County Registry of Deeds, Ellsworth, Maine"

A four-hundred-ninety-acre segment was the theoretical amount to be set aside. This was the initial acreage to be legally granted Hannah for her utilization. While other portions were being sold off, this plot would ideally remain untouched. It would take an action of the court to "release the dower" in order for it to be acquired by another. Debtors could not lay claim to that property without the release.

The Widow's Dower

Until the 1890s, the state of Massachusetts and then the state of Maine supported legislation designed to protect a widow from abject poverty upon the death of her husband. A portion encompassing up to one-third of the land was set aside, known as "the widow's dower." It could not be sold or taken over by another interest until her death. Land ownership was considered the only substantial means of sustainability. Thus, as the widow now owned this land for her use, she should be able, through wise management or sale, to support herself and her children, should she not remarry. Even if she marries again, the "dower" remains at her disposal.

Appeals were made, however, to reduce the acreage of the dower because debts required further sale of assets. The evidence to suggest appeals succeeded is seen in the map above. A section lying just north of Little Long Pond, including Jordan Brook and points east, ultimately made up the dower for Hannah. It had shrunk to just under twenty acres.

V

BEATEN DOWN, LIFE RESURGES

Those who remained of the original families from the shores of Jordan Pond found a way to continue, despite hardships, setbacks, and disappointment.

JORDAN FAMILY MEMBERS

Alden

When Alden returned from Massachusetts, he lived with his family on Little Cranberry Island. Full-time work eventually ended at the Jordan mill. Alden acquired the task of lighthouse keeper on Baker Island from 1867-1870. During that time he proceeded to administer the estate of his late father. With some luck, he would be able to support his family and continue paying down his own debts. He eventually became a harbormaster, maneuvering many a ship through the archipelago to its destination. Sea captains brought him gifts from afar in gratitude for this truly remarkable skill.

Abbie

Abbie had moved shortly after Alden did, following him to Massachusetts. She married James Connant of Saugus, in March of 1851, just before her twenty-first birthday. In February of 1854, she gave birth to Ina Maud, her only daughter. Her husband was enlisted in the local militia. A bizarre accident happened in September 1856. At target practice his commanding officer's musket misfired and killed James, right there on the range. Abbie later remarried and is recorded as an heir in the George Jordan estate as Abbie Austin of Massachusetts.

John S. Jordan

Several years after Lucy died, John married Olive Moore in the fall of 1869. He brought her to the house on the pond to live for the few remaining years. Mill operations slowed to almost a standstill. He continued to eke out a meager living. The local judge had to defer to a higher court which had jurisdiction over John's boundary line case. Resolution was reached with the help of local commissioners. He was able to begin relinquishment of the property to a local speculator. By 1880, Charles How began that process of ownership transfer. It would take three years. During that time, John made arrangements to move to Ellsworth, his neighbors being sad to see him go. John's daughters stayed in the area, marrying young men from Northeast Harbor and Ellsworth. Philena had one daughter before she passed away at the age of twenty-nine. Elizabeth lived a long life on the mainland, raising three daughters. They all stayed in the region, raising John's great grandchildren. John passed away on May 26, 1890, at the age of seventy-six.

Hannah Jordan Bracy and her Children

Hannah's daughter Cedelia had married John Clement at seventeen and had a son, Edwin. They lived in the village of Seal Harbor, helping out John's father and uncle with the inn they were building. By then the summer visitor population had out-grown the Clement boarding house. But Cedie died in July 1870. Three years later her child died as well. Her husband, John Clement, is listed among the heirs to the George N. Jordan estate.

Melvina died shortly after giving birth to her son, Melvin, in 1865, at age sixteen. Melvin is listed as co-heir.

Alice Jane lived with her husband George Bracy, her stepfather's son, and a seaman. Life by the sea was rugged, but she was used to it, having spent her young teens in the Bracy household. She was content there along the coast, caring for her newborn child. Her husband spent long stretches, as did most offshore fishermen, away from home. She would visit her mother and sister during those lonely days. Then came the day when her husband's ship returned without him. George had been lost at sea. Eventually her health began to fail. She died three months after her eighteenth birthday, in August 1870. The whole Bracy family mourned with her. And her child, Sidney Bracy, listed as co-heir of the estate, became another child Hannah would raise.

It is heart-wrenching to realize two of Hannah's three daughters died within two months of each other in 1870. None would live into their twenties.

George Jr. and His Progeny

The only remaining child of George Newbegin, Sr. and Hannah was my great-grandfather, George "Junior." As a young adult he excelled in the carpentry trade and, as you may imagine, in offshore fishing. He grew to manhood among the Bracy sailors. He also got acquainted with Captain Stanley from Little Cran-berry Island. George sailed with those crews to the Florida Keys and the Caribbe-an. He went fishing with Captain Stanley in the wintertime, out toward the Grand Banks. George Junior's expedition went out from the large vessel on a smaller craft. He kept careful records on a slate of the poundage of fish brought back to the ves-sels. The slate recounted his share of the catch and thus his wages from the work. That year, Junior turned twenty-one. Records state he was able to purchase the pond from Alden who was still administrator of their father's estate.

Not long after that, George Junior began courting a young lady from Islesford, named Eunice Carrie Stanley. No doubt she was related to his captain. George began preparations for settling down by building a home on the outskirts of Seal Harbor.

George finished the place just in time. The couple was married on Christmas Eve, 1880. George and Carrie—that is what she went by—would live out their lives raising eight children to adulthood. He continued to ply the trade of carpentry and offshore fishing throughout his life. Conch shells from the West Indies lined the windowsills. Solidly built tables, benches, and cabinets graced their home. All these, now memorabilia, bestowed a love for the sea and of building to his children and grandchildren.

When Captain Bracy passed in 1883, George looked after his mother. That was the year George and Carrie's first child, Everett, was born. Hannah would occupy her mind and heart with the little one. Hannah Jordan Bracy had outlived two husbands and her three daughters. Putting her mind to work with the infant probably helped to soften her memories. Everett grew up to be a plumber. He married a local gal named Esther and they raised Alice and John. He operated the small plumbing supply store in town. Everett provided plumbing service to the Rockefeller family estate, known as The Eyrie.

Edwin appeared the next year. "Eddie" became a livery and a courier. He and his wife, Mary, raised Colgate. He also supplied the villagers with a regular store of firewood and refrigeration ice from Jordan Pond. He often recruited the help of his grandsons Stewart and Frank, nephew George, and a few boys from the village. He became the sport of hilarious memories for those youngsters who helped him with his duties but sometimes were paid with a mere cold glass of water.

Cora came along in 1886, and the house was bursting at the seams. George took to expanding their living space, adding an addition to the home there along Bracy Cove. Cora became a teacher and served in a local hotel in summers. She later stepped away from teaching in order to help her mother Carrie live out her years there along the shore.

George Millard, born in 1888, sadly died at the age of two. An infant born in 1890, lived only a month. Epidemics of the late 1800s continued the cycle of grief and resurgence for so many families in Maine, theirs included.

It wasn't long before Lena was born, then Ina, George Milton, Myra in 1901, and finally Francis Leon Jordan in 1905. In Hannah's later years, she continued helping to look after the children as well as being looked after by them.

Lena married Loring Watson and raised a family of five. She became Seal Harbor's telephone operator as well as a service entrepreneur, washing laundry and ironing linens for the well-to-do summer folk. Ina followed Cora and became a history teacher. She taught the children on Little Cranberry, Baker Island, Great Cranberry, and others. Remaining single, Ina moved to Manchester, New Hampshire, and completed her teaching career there. Summers she returned to

Mount Desert and occupied the home at Seal Harbor with her sister Cora and her mother Carrie. After the others had passed, Ina would continue to return in the summers. Over afternoon tea, she would enjoy telling stories to her nieces, nephews, grandnieces, and grandnephews. Times of sitting for the Rockefellers, looking after Nelson and David. Telling stories of John D.'s kindness to her father and how their friendly acquaintance got on as both men aged.

Mr. Rockefeller kept in touch with George's children, even grandchildren, including sending congratulations to my grandmother Myra upon her college graduation and a gift for her wedding. He stayed in touch with her in-laws, the Sanborns, and even sent congratulations to my mother, Carolyn, on the occasion of her wedding.

Ina was the last living relative to occupy the Jordan house on Bracy Cove. John D.'s son David Rockefeller bought the home in 1964 to preserve the area, happy for the Jordans to continue to occupy the place for as long as they needed. In 1978, after Ina's passing, the house was moved slightly east to enhance an adjoining property. The old Jordan land now features a rail-fenced area for horses, a family garden, and a sweeping view of the cove.

Milton and my grandmother Myra were the two who left the island, married, and would raise families elsewhere in Maine. Milton would settle in Millinocket, pursuing a career in the front office of the papermill industry. He married Clara Jones and had three children. Myra married Ralph Sanborn, of Wales, who became a successful potato and dairy farmer. They raised four children. Myra contracted cancer and died in 1950. Ralph never remarried, continuing to farm until shortly before his passing in 1993.

Francis Leon never married. He became a lobsterman, his boat anchored right offshore from the home on Bracy Cove. He occupied a room above the kitchen, having a window to the sea. He used the carriage house (still seen along Route 3, Peabody Drive) as his shop and lobster trap storage.

Carriage House turned Lobster shack occupied by Francis Jordan until the 1950s.
Photo courtesy of Carolyn Reeverts.

As he would set out early in the morning, a tamed gull would fly over and set upon the stern. Francis would feed it from his bait bucket as he prepared the traps for deployment. It became a faithful pet, flying behind the boat then, trap to trap, landing astern waiting for a handout.

This common sight along the island harbors blends with fantasy in the children's storybook *Burt Dow, Deep-Water Man* by Robert McCloskey.

Francis became the stuff of his own legend among his nephews and nieces with his mysterious winter disappearances to Ellsworth. Sometimes he would return to Seal Harbor late at night by taxi. He would run inside to borrow money from Cora in order to pay the driver. Now and then, Cora would get so put out by her brother, she would close off the heat to his room that came from the kitchen woodstove! Each spring he would start up his lobstering with a little financial help from his brother Milton.

THE FINAL GOODBYE

It was in late 1880 that the old farmhouse on Jordan Pond, built by George and John, was occupied by Mr. Melvin Tibbets of Exeter, Maine. He ran a small business there which offered modest meals, stables, and boat rentals. By late 1883 the land was in the hands of Charles How, a realtor from Boston. Mr. How admired this setting so much he would often bring prospective clients to picnic on the lawn. Charles eventually sold the house to Thomas McIntire and his wife. The McIntires opened the teahouse in 1895 and operated it under the name, "The Jordan Pond House." This has been its title ever since.

Hannah lived to see her home on Jordan Pond well used as a tea house. She watched as the wealthy summer people made a way for it and the island to become a place of respite and rejuvenation. Beginning in 1911 the surrounding area was gradually conveyed to the United States. She was present, thanks to her grandchildren, to witness the opening of Sieur de Monts National Monument in 1916.

Hannah passed away December 28th, 1916 at the age of ninety-two.

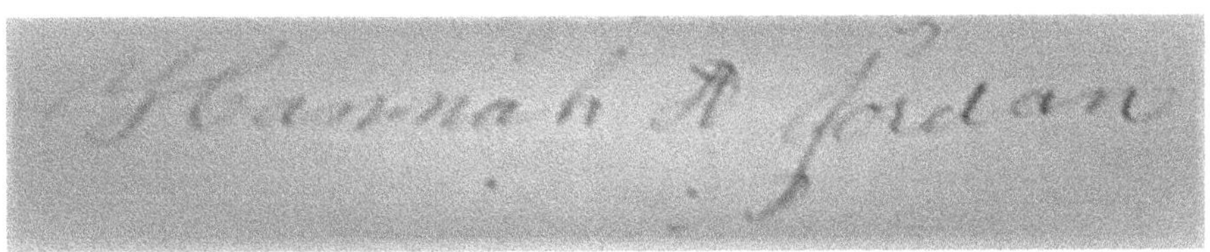

HANNAH'S SIGNATURE is taken from a document in the Probate records of Hancock County in Ellsworth, Maine. It is the only record found in her own handwriting. Unfortunately, no photographs or other writing has been found from her or her late husband. If only a diary, a journal, or a photo was available, how much richer the story would be.

The area became Lafayette National Park in 1919 and renamed Acadia National Park in 1929. Hannah's former home itself became part of the park by 1940, bequeathed to the United States by John D. Rockefeller, Jr.

CONCLUSION

So, after all the research and puzzling over the details, I realized what I had uncovered. Or more accurately, what I hadn't. It actually was not the threat of Mr. Dorr's actions that my relatives fell victim to. Mr. Dorr was closer to the age of the son George Junior, ramping up his land trust donations after 1900.

Pressure from the influx of wealthy families after 1840 did transform the area around Seal Harbor, Jordan Pond, and the rest of Mount Desert Island. My great-great-grandfather's enterprise of the 1840s, however, predated the assembly of the Hancock County Trustees of Public Reservation of 1901. Yet the irony remains. In the midst of a park built upon acquiring land at the expense of local logging efforts stands an enduring tribute … to a lumberman.

Upon the Jordan Pond House's re-opening after the devastating fire of 1979, David Rockefeller, Jr. reflected in his speech:

> *"Acadia's most enduring symbol has been, I believe, the Jordan Pond House."*[14]

An enduring symbol, to be sure. A symbol for an enduring, albeit obscure, family as well. For there was something else I discovered. The Jordans didn't consider themselves victims. *Percussa Resurgo: Beaten down, I rise again.* Harsh realities of nineteenth-century life were understood as inevitable. These were met with determination, ingenuity, perseverance, and a sense of community. In the end, the family moved on and thrived in other ways—along the shores of Seal Harbor and beyond.

Jordan Pond is a locale of international fame. It holds a cherished sentiment for the Jordan family, as you might expect. When I visit or work along its shores, I cannot help but pause for just a moment. Through the early morning mist rising from the waters, I listen for the echoes of crashing timber, of a waterwheel and a millrace. I pick my steps, casually perusing the streambed for artifacts. A clump of hardened sawdust, maybe a broken sawtooth. Alas, these exist only in our family's collective memory. As I stand by this peaceful landscape, I pause to consider a long-forgotten legacy.

---

[14] David B. Woodside, *The Story of Jordan Pond* (Bar Harbor, ME: Acadia Corporation, 1996), 10.

Making a way for a family, during tough times or fair, means taking risks, trusting God, taking nothing for granted. It is a legacy worth remembering. *Percussa Resurgo*; skill, humility, and will; remain grateful but determined and, '*when knocked off our horse, best a* [modern-day proverbial] *Saracen*' and press on.

ACKNOWLEDGMENTS

There are a number of persons responsible for the insights, stories, references, and technical assistance that made this publication possible. I am greatly indebted to each of them. It has been a delight to explore the family line of my maternal grandmother, Myra E. Jordan, known only from the recollections of my mother, Carolyn Reeverts, since Grandmother Jordan passed in 1950. From the extended family of the Jordans, I have appreciated the conversations, hospitality, and conviviality of Mom's relatives: my cousins Cathy and Steve Roy, Mom's sister Marilyn Greenwood, her cousin George Jordan, his sister Louise Jordan Anderson, and my second cousin, Louise's daughter, Patti Gervais. There are other relatives who have supplied interesting and specific details: Frank Jordan, Cheryl Watson, and Dr. Vernard Adams. My research was enhanced through the support of the team at Acadia National Park Archives in 2014; Tim Garrity of the Mount Desert Historical Society; Deborah Dyer, director of Bar Harbor Historical Society; Ann Funderbunk and her husband Lance of Seal Harbor's Public Library; Hannah Stephens and the late Robert Pyle of Northeast Harbor Library; Mount Desert Deputy and Town Clerks Jennifer Buchanan and Claire Woolfolk; The Friends of Acadia; scholars at the University of Maine in Orono: Dr. Melvin Johnson, librarian, Raymond H. Fogler Library, and his assistant, Desiree Butterfield-Nagy, M.L.I.S. of the Special Collections Department, and Dr. Richard Judd, professor of history; Peter Jones and Jill Ryder who worked with me at the Jordan Pond House; Patten Lumberman's Museum curators and volunteers; the late Tony Sohns, wildlife biologist and natural history educator who inspired more than the children that day at Ellsworth Public Library. My research into 1840s sawmills was influenced by Frank Maciejewski, engineer and town historian, who patiently, over several years of visits, talked me through the design and construction of the Hurd & Briggs 1846 Sawmill in Elma, New York—including the many potential dangers associated with mill work. My research into wildfire history on Mount Desert Island was sparked by Kent Nelson, forest ranger specialist of Maine's Forest Service when he got me in touch with William A. Patterson III, professor emeritus, University of Massachusetts, Amherst. Many thanks, Kent! Professor Patterson's research and publications provided important insight into corroborating the varying accounts of wildfires in and around Jordan Pond in the nineteenth century. I am indebted to Roger Paul, a language specialist of the Passamaquoddy Nation from Pleasant town, Maine. His wealth of knowledge, insight, advocacy for Native American culture and tradition throughout New England is truly remarkable; a great deal of my understanding of the Wabanaki sense of place I gained through Roger's influence. I appreciate the support and suggestions provided by my friend and co-worker in education, author Wendy Dunham, as well as Anne and Dusty Warner, fellow Interpretive Rangers from Acadia National Park. I appreciate the technical assistance and invaluable suggestions from Andrea Merrell and Ann Tatlock. The time and focus needed to put this in writing came about through the hospitality of my friends Katherine Fernald, Bud and Melanie Campbell, and Kathy Bishop; my parents, Daryl and Carolyn Reeverts, my brother, Dan Reeverts, my aunt, Marilyn Greenwood, my son, Thomas Reeverts, and his family. I've been blessed by the artistic passion and ability of Thomas and my longtime friend Robert P. Kline, who have graciously characterized portions of this record with their work. Finally, two individuals to whom I attribute supplying great motivation at key points in the timeline are my writing coach and author Eddie Jones who assisted me in the final stages, and Melanie Ruark, fellow Teacher Ranger, veteran literacy teacher and Native American Literacy Project specialist, and dear friend who encouraged me to get this project started in the first place. Thank you and God bless you!

APPENDIX A

Suggestions for Further Reading

Four Generations in Maine: The Carroll Family of Southwest Harbor 1825-1917 by Henry Raup. Eastern National. 1993.

Historic Acadia National Park, The Stories behind one of America's Great Treasures by Catherine Schmitt. Lyons Press. 2016.

Indians in Eden: Wabanakis and Rusticators on Maine's Mount Desert Island 1840s – 1920s by Bunny McBride and Harald E.L. Prins. Downeast Books. 2009.

John Gilley One of the Forgotten Millions by Charles Eliot. Acadia Publishing (reprint edition) 1989.

The Story of Acadia by George B. Dorr. Acadia Publishing. (3rd ed.) 1997.

The Story of Jordan Pond by David B. Woodside. Acadiacorp. 1989

The Story of Mount Desert Island by Samuel Eliot Morison. Islandport Press. (2nd ed.) 2011.

Suggestions for Exploration

Abbe Museum *https://www.abbemuseum.org/*

Abby Aldrich Rockefeller Garden – Land & Garden Preserve *https://www. gardenpreserve/plan- your-visit*

Acadia National Park *https://www.nps.gov/acad/index.htm*

Bar Harbor Historical Society *https://barharborhistorical.org*

Frenchman's Bay Conservancy *https://frenchmanbay.org/*

Jordan Pond Buoy *www.jpbuoy.com*

Jordan Pond House *www.jordanpondhouse.com*

Mount Desert Island Historical Society *mdihistory.org*

Mount Desert Island Preserves - Maine Coast Heritage Trust *https://www.mcht. org/visit-a-preserve/regions/mount-desert-island/*

Patten Lumbermen's Museum *https://lumbermensmuseum.org*

Wendell Gilley Museum *https://www.wendellgilleymuseum.org*

1840's sawmill reproduction & history: *https://www.youtube.com/watch?v=ta-aVqyGd7Oo*

DVD: *Dancing At the Mill: Two Centuries of Life on Mount Desert Island.* Dobbs Productions. 2011.

APPENDIX B

Additional Photos

Photographs have yet to be found of George N. Jordan (Sr.), John S. Jordan, or their wives.

Original Jordan House circa 1898 with added dining room and veranda. The section on the left is the original farmhouse. Photo courtesy Northeast Harbor Library Archives.

The original farmhouse section with porch added. Photo from The Bar Harbor Times, June 28, 1979. "Loss of Jordan Pond House," Northeast Harbor Library, accessed October 23, 2019, https://nehl.digitalarchive.us/ items/show/1217. Item 2211."

Jordan Pond circa 1890.

Jordan Pond, Autumn, 2021.

George Jordan (Jr) home on Bracy Cove. Circa 1900. Photo courtesy of Seal Harbor Library.

Jordan's Seal Harbor house on Bracy Cove, circa 1965.

Seal Harbor's Bracy Cove, continued:

Francis's Lobster boat. Note the gulls trailing behind.

Post Card courtesy of Carolyn Reeverts.

Tourists these days unknowingly pass right by the property where the house once sat on the shore of Bracy Cove. It stood just east of the cobblestone seawall on route three, a natural seawall across from Little Long Pond. Back then the road was a dirt path to Northeast Harbor, with a wooden bridge over the stream that flows from the pond to the cove.

Second generation photos

George Jordan (Jr) and Carrie Stanley wedding photos 1880. Photo courtesy of Patti Gervais.

George and Carrie 50th Anniversary. 1930. Photo courtesy of Patti Gervais.

1979 FIRE AT JORDAN POND HOUSE

Bangor Daily News, June 22, 1979, courtesy Special Collections Department, Raymond H Fogler Library, University of Maine, Orono, Maine.

By Christopher Spruce
NEWS Hancock Bureau

SEAL HARBOR — It had survived the Bar Harbor fire of 1947. But in a little more than two hours Thursday morning, the 132-year-old Jordan Pond House, famous the world over for its tea and popovers, was destroyed by fire of an undetermined origin.

The fire, which erased the last vestige of a bygone era, apparently began in the gift shop area of the wood-frame complex about 6:50 a.m.

"It's always been a potential hazard because we knew the building was a tinderbox," said Kenneth Goodyear, executive vice president of the Acadia Corp., the concessionaire which leases the Jordan Pond House from the U.S. Park Service.

"We always considered this the ultimate possible 'disaster," said Goodyear.

Park Ranger Stan Robins said more than a dozen summer employees housed in a dormitory in the building were awakened by a smoke detector and tried unsuccessfully to contain the fire using buckets of water and fire extinguishers.

See JORDAN on Page 2

The Bar Harbor Times excerpts courtesy of Northeast Harbor Library Archives, Northeast Harbor, Maine

Acadia National Park Fire Control Chief Roger Rudolph and National Park Service Regional Safety Inspector Joe Wedland dig for clues in the charred rubble.

PAGE TWO - The Bar Harbor Times, Thursday, June 28, 1979

POPOVERS
[Continued from Page 1]

Park the same day explained that a study team from the regional park service, based in Boston, would be analyzing alternatives for the Jordan Pond site. White listed five possibilities to be considered.

One is the restoration of the Pond House building, the idea decided upon by Acadia Corporation.

Another possibility is to establish an interpretive display of the traditions and history of Jordan Pond House. White explained that the Interpretive Design Center of the National Park System based in Harpers Ferry W.V. had already drawn up plans for such a display prior to the fire.

The Superintendent mentioned, too, the idea of a special building for cross country skiing. Rebuilding the House for limited use only, for instance popovers and tea only, is also possible.

Lastly, White said the Jordan Pond land could be returned to nature.

The Superintendent said the decision would be made by himself and the North Atlantic Regional Director Jack Stark, but that ultimately the Director of the National Park Service in Washington, William Whalen, and the Secretary of the Interior, William Andrews, could influence the results.

Any alternative involving a large sum of money would take at least three years to process through the Department of the Interior Parks and Recreation budget, White said.

Another park option is to contract out the job of rebuilding, give the contractor possessory interest and give the Park the title.

White could not be reached by press time Wednesday to respond to the summer proposal from Acadia Corporation, but according to Kenneth Goodyear, the Superintendent has been approached with the idea and will be considering it during the next few days.

Petitions asking the National Park Service to rebuild the Jordan Pond House have garnered over 1300 signatures around the Island. The document placed in Acadia Corporation's 85 Main St. shop by Edwin Garrett contained some 490 names from across the nation, and some interesting comments as well. One woman called the House "a major drawing card for visitors to the Island," and a Bettsville, Md. resident stated, "Acadia without the Pond House is like New York without the Statue of Liberty."

One of the longer comments came from Bar Harbor citizen Elisabeth (Mrs. R. Amory) Thorndike who captured the feeling of many restoration proponents by writing that "Jordan Pond House existed and succeeded because of its magnificent setting, still exactly as it was 132 years ago. They graciousness of its hospitality made for worldwide friends and the best possible public relations for the National Park Service. Acadia National Park revived after the tragic fire of 1947, and so can Jordan Pond House."

In Northeast Harbor, nearly 300 persons had signed by Wednesday morning. The petition's organizer there, Hannah Garrett, told of a dramatic illustration of a woman who when asked to sign, said she liked it the way it was. Having just arrived in town, she'd not heard of the fire. When Hannah explained, the woman fainted and fell to the floor. Coming to, seconds later, she signed gladly.

Southwest Harbor petitions contained around 500 signatures by mid-day Wednesday. Petition collector Richard Homer voiced the opinion: "It's the only park in the country that was given to the National Park Service by the people...the people are now saying the Jordan Pond House should be rebuilt."

BAR HARBOR TIMES

Second Class Postage paid at Bar Harbor, Maine

USPS - 044-060

Issue of June 28, 1979

Published Every Thursday

The Bar Harbor Times, Thursday, June 28, 1979 - PAGE TWENTY-ONE

Island Mourns Loss Of Jordan Pond House

Firefighters Battle A Tinder-Box Blaze

The tragic fire that destroyed the Jordan Pond House was discovered shortly after 6:42 a.m. June 26th when a smoke alarm sounded in the dormitory building where 12 staff members were sleeping.

Running downstairs to the breezeway between the two buildings, Steward Georgitis was the first to reach the fire. Looking through the gift shop door into the smoke filled room, he saw what he thought was the flame center near the eastern wall. Smoke was escaping from under the door. Attempting to turn the door knob, he burned his hand. As he turned back towards the porch and kitchen entrance, he heard glass cracking.

By this time two other staff members, Mike Raynor and Megan McCarthy were reporting the fire from pay phones. The one in the office was dead and the one in the gift shop was unreachable.

Before running back to the men's quarters in a nearby cottage for change, Raynor alerted staff members, making certain they all had left the dorm. Fortunately Megan had the correct change but there must have been some difficulty in locating the correct phone number which is listed under Mt. Desert Fire Department. Apparently thinking she was calling Seal Harbor, she reached the dispatcher in Northeast Harbor at 6:50 and informed him there was a "large fire" in the gift shop.

Immediately the dispatcher, Peter Bucklin, blew the alarm to summons Northeast Harbor volunteer firemen, simultaneously notifying the Seal Harbor volunteer department.

Seal Harbor Fire Chief Jack Tracy reports that by the time his first fire truck reached the Jordan Pond House, the flames were already through the windows of the gift shop, reaching up the outside walls.

He says "it was one of the fastest responses I've ever seen. The truck was moving even before the whistle was in high gear." The call came in at 6:50 and the two Seal Harbor fire trucks were on the scene by 6:55. A Northeast Harbor fire truck arrived five minutes later.

Hose was laid from the Pond House to the Seal Harbor pumper stationed at Jordan Pond 1,000 feet away and the trucks were positioned in front of the building. Realizing more assistance was needed, Tracy called for a second Northeast Harbor truck and the Otter Creek tanker (One of the Somesville trucks was dispatched to Northeast Harbor to cover that area).

In the meantime, Georgitis had grabbed a CO2 fire extinguisher from the kitchen, and pushed the funnel through the upper door panels which had broken by then. Before it was half empty, some of the windows had cracked, flames leaking from the top of them.

For the next few minutes, until the extinguisher was depleted, he used it on the outside wall to contain the fire as it was coming through the window tops.

Other staff members, clad in bathrobes, joined him in the breezeway, formed a bucket brigade with plastic ice cream containers and threw water on the fire.

Shortly afterwards, Georgitis recalls, the fire department arrived and began shooting

[Continued on Page 21]

Hendricks Photo

Routine Inspection Turns Investigation

Joseph Wadland, Safety Specialist for the Northern Atlantic Region of the National Park Service, arrived in Bar Harbor on Wednesday, June 18. He and two other Park Service personnel were to start Thursday on a follow-up safety inspection at the Jordan Pond House in Seal Harbor and the Civilian Conservation Corps. buildings on McFarland's Hill in Bar Harbor.

The three inspectors were to follow up on a routine OSHA inspection made a month earlier at the Acadia Corpora-

[Continued on Page 36]

Cause Unknown In First Report
Early Morning Jogger, Gardener See No Fire

The first official investigation report issued Tuesday from Acadia National Park headquarters offers a specific point of origin for the fire which consumed the Jordan Pond House, but can list only possible but unlikely causes. The final classification of probable cause is "unknown."

The preliminary report was issued by Acadia National Park Fire Control Officer Roger Rudolph and National Park Service Safety Inspector Joseph Wadland. They began talking to witnesses and

[Continued on Page 36]

The Passing Of An Era
By Russell D. Butcher

My first shocked reaction was, "Uh, my God, it's gone!" My wife and I and the Rev. and Mrs. Douglas Morrill, were just returning from a week in Canada. With no prior warning, we rounded the bend in the mountain road of Acadia National Park, and suddenly saw the flattened, burned ruins of what for generations had been the beloved Jordan Pond House. It was the day following the fire—and the three great fireplace chimneys and burned ovens rose grotesquely above the ashes.

As with so many people on Mt. Desert and throughout the United States, we feel stunned, numb and empty. Our minds simply refuse to accept what we see with our eyes. We literally grieve for the passing of an old friend. The loss closes forever a historical era that embraced many generations of tea-and-popover devotees. It will be a long time before my wife and I won't automatically think: "Let's go for a hike and end up at the Jordan Pond House for some fresh peach ice cream and popovers."

The Jordan Pond House began in 1847 as a modest little farmhouse built by George N. and John Stanley Jordan of the nearby village of Seal Harbor. They planted a small apple orchard, and conducted a logging operation with a small sawmill and dam at the outlet of Jordan Pond. The farmhouse narrowly survived the "Great Fire" of 1864 that burned an extensive area of surrounding forest.

In 1896, Melvan Tibbetts and his family of Exeter, Maine, bought the Jordan farm, and that summer a small advertisement was placed in the Mount Desert Herald proclaiming that "a full line of first class boats and canoes" could be found at the pond, plus "good stabling and feed for horses. Parties crossing

Marcia Rocke Photo

[Continued on Page 25]

MAINE-ISMS

Phrases and Words of Maine's Vernacular: A Collection of Sayings in the Public Domain

PHRASES

Blinkah fluid: Something Mainers accuse tourists of forgetting to fill before visiting.

Breezed up: When Maine weather gets windy. "*My, my, it's breezed up outside!*"

By Godfrey: Phrase; Affirmative in the extreme.

Darker than a pocket: No light; "*Jeezum, it's darker than a pocket in this attic!*"

Down cellar: or "Down cellah." Where you go to put things "in the basement."

Drove right up: Busy; "*At Christmas we're drove right up, so it may take longer.*" (See also, "right out straight.")

Eighteen-hundred-and-froze-to-death: The period of 1816-17, one of the worst winters Maine ever experienced; "*Jeezum, it ain't been this cold since Eighteen-hundred-and-froze-to-death!*"

Finest kind: Used variously, as a general sign of approval; also used ironically; "*That was an awesome dinner; finest kind.*"

From away: People who are not native-born in Maine. *"Don't mind him, he's from away."*

Glob around: To relax or chill out; *"We went up to camp and just globbed around all weekend."*

Hard tellin' not knowin': In other words, "I don't know."

No bigger than a fart in a mitten: Tiny; *"Aww, look at her, she's no bigger than a fart in a mitten!"*

Number than a hake: More colorful way to say someone is stupid; *"I tell you, that kid across the street is number than a hake."*

Right out straight: Very busy, non-stop busyness. *"I'm sorry, sir; you can't talk to the owner, he's right out straight this evening. Try calling back tomorrow."* (See also, "drove right up.")

Stove up: To wipe out, flounder, or crash. *"The best place to watch canoes 'stove it up' is at the second rapids."*

Up Country: Usually a location, cabin, or otherwise north of Millinocket or Greenville, where fishing, hunting, and snowmobiling can occur, often unhindered.

You can't get there from here: "You can't get theyah from heeah" – A saying meaning there's no way to get directly to the desired destination from the current location (without going either back the previous direction or round about and way out of the way). Or, more likely, in jest, truly meaning you can't get there from here.

WORDS

Apiece: A ways away—an undetermined distance. *"Down the road apiece."*

Auguster: The State Capitol, "Augusta." Usually, words ending in vowels get an *r* attached to the ending, while words ending in *r* typically lose the *r* and in its place get the *ah* sound (try it yourself on another example: Banana becomes *bananer*; car becomes *cah*).

Ayuh: Yes, uh huh; affirmative; *"Ayuh, that's the right address but you've got the wrong person."*

Barvel: A fisherman's apron made of leather or oilcloth; *"When they measured the lobsters, the water splashed over their barvels and into their faces."*

Beater: (Beetah) An old car used in winter or an old, unregistered vehicle that usually gets beat up while hauling just about anything.

Big'uns: Large ones of whatever. *"Did you catch any fish?" "Ayuh, I got two big'uns."*

Blinkkah: Quite confusing for some. You see, those from away, although they never use them themselves, refer to this as a "turn signal" or sometimes a "directional light." In Maine, it's called a "Blinkkah" (blinker). With the strong influence of the French Canadians in Maine, a blinkkah is a difficult concept to understand. Once a man in an IGA parking lot was having some difficulty with his and asked a passerby if he could tell him if his blinkkah was working. In a very thick French accent the man replied, "Ayuh, nope, ayuh, nope, ayuh, nope..."
    - Contributed by *Laugh Maine* (from Bethel, Maine)

Bubbler: Water fountain.

Bureau: Where one stores one's clothes. (See also, "Chestadraws.")

Carriage: The cart you use to wheel your groceries around at grocery stores, such as Hannaford's.

Chestadraws: Where clothes are stored in one's bedroom. (See also, "Bureau.")

Chimbly: The place where the smoke goes up from the woodstove. *"There's smoke a-risin' from the chimbly, they must be home."*

Culch: Any kind of trash or rubbish; occasionally used of a person held in low esteem; *"I'm gonna clean all that culch of the basement if it's the last thing I do!"*

Cuff: A verb meaning to slap up the side of the hairline. *"Jimmy's mom cuffed him for sassing his Aunt Barbara."*

Cunnin': Cute, adorable; *"Her daughter is so cunnin'!"*

Cussid: Cursed, obstinate; *"This cussid car won't start up!"*

Dite: As in, "just a dite"—meaning, just a little. Someone might ask if you want whipped cream on a dessert and you'd say, *"Oh, just a dite."*

Dooryard: The front yard of a house or establishment; an area immediately next to the front door of a house; *"That fella drove over the curb and right up into the dooryard."*

Dry-ki: Dead timber, especially that which was caused by flooding; dry branches; driftwood; land where such timber predominates; *"Don't build a fire there, there's way too much dri-ki."*

Dub: A stupid person; plural, dubbers; *"Those guys are a bunch of dubbers."*

Elastic: Otherwise known as a rubber band. *"Let me put an elastic around those pens to hold them."*

Fog mull: A heavy, stationary fog bank; *"That fog mull rolled in wicked fast, and now I can't see anything."*

Frappe: A milkshake or malted drink. Typically made up of ice cream, milk and chocolate syrup blended. The *e* is silent.

Gaumy: Awkward, inept, stupid; *"Look at him singing karaoke, what a gaumy dub he is!"*

Glom: To grab, or to be greedy; "*She glommed up all the leftover candy.*"

Greasy: When roads are "icy" or "slippery."

Groaners: A whistling buoy or foghorn; "*Those groaners are driving me crazy; I jump each time they sound off!*"

Idear: A thought, as in "I have an idear!" It's another example of the unique Maine vernacular idiosyncrasy: Idea PLUS an *r*. Sometimes actually spoken or mimicked by people from away as "I-dee-ah," as if it's really spelled with an *r*!

> "Did you ever hear the story about the two Maine kids who were studying for a spelling bee? When they got to 'idea,' they puzzled for a while, and then one turned to the other and said, 'I know, you spell it just like it is pronounced, only the *r* is silent.'" – contributor: Lynda Wiener

Italians: Uniquely made sandwiches much like what are often known as submarine sandwiches or subs.

Jeezum crow: Or just, "**Jeezum**." Mild expletive: "*Jeezum crow, I thought you were going to run into that car!*"

Jimmies: Little chocolate or multi-colored sprinkles the attendant at the ice cream store puts on top of an ice cream cone.

Katahdin: Mount Katahdin is the northern terminus of the Appalachian Trail, located in Baxter State Park, west of Millinocket, Maine. There really is no *r* in Katahdin. But if you ask an old-time Mainer how it would sound if it *did* have an *r* in the middle of its name…

Kife: To "steal"; "*I think he was planning to kife that lure.*"

Larrigan: A type of long-legged moccasin or boot; "*Throw on those larrigans and grab your fishing pole!*"

Larrup: To give or receive a beating; "*You kids settle down or you're gonna get a good larrup!*"

Laury: Describes overcast weather; "*It's been laury out today.*"

Leaf Peepers: A humorous description of tourists arriving after Labor Day.

Money cat: A calico cat, especially one with at least three colors; "*Aunt Marilyn's new kitten is a money cat; she's a cute one.*"

Moxie: 1: Energy, pep; 2: Courage, determination; 3: Know-how, ability. But in Maine? It's the name of a once-locally produced soft drink.

Did you know? Courtesy of Merriam-Webster Inc.

"Hot roasted peanuts! Fresh popcorn! Ice-cold Moxie!" You might have heard such a snack vendor's cry at a baseball game—if you attended it in 1924. That was the heyday of the soft drink named "Moxie," which some claim outsold Coca-Cola at the height of its popularity. The beverage was a favorite of American writer E. B. White, who wrote, "Moxie contains gentian root, which is the path to the good life. This was known in the second century before Christ and is a boon to me today." By 1930, "moxie" had become a slang term for nerve and verve, perhaps because some people thought the drink was a tonic that could cure virtually any ill and bring vim and vigor back to even the most lethargic individual."[15]

Mug-up: When you've eaten so much, you're really full…

Numb: Stupid; "*What, are you numb? Put that down!*"

Orts: Scraps left at a table, to be given to pigs; "*I'll gather up the orts and take them out back.*"

Pekid: To get or to look "sick." "*That child looks a little pekid.*"

Plague: A verb meaning to curse. "*Ol' Joe he plagued that pond and ain't nothin' been caught since!*"

---

[15] "Moxie Definition & Meaning," Merriam-Webster (Merriam-Webster), accessed February 17, 2016, https://www.merriam-webster.com/dictionary/moxie.

Ploye: Traditional Acadian buckwheat pancake; *"Ployes with butter and maple syrup are delicious."*

Pregnant for: To be pregnant, as opposed to "pregnant with"; *"When I was pregnant for Erin, whoopie pies were what I would binge on."*

Puckerbrush: A thicket of alders, but also used for a briar patch, or other nasty underbrush one must maneuver through for some reason.

Pull-haul: To argue, contend; *"They pull-hauled the problem over all night long."*

Putty: Also, with "around"; to occupy oneself with trifles, to idle; *"He was puttying around with the lawn mower all day."*

Rig: Flamboyant personality; *"His sister was a bit of a rig, always needing the attention."*

Riley: Used to describe the color of the ocean after a big storm; *"The bay was all riley this morning."*

Scrid: Tiny portion; *"All that was left of the soup was the scrids. And I was hungry!"*

Scrod: Fish served which featured a method of salting and preserving codfish; *"We had beans, coffee, and some scrod for supper."*

Showah: A Mainer's accent for the word sure.

Short: An illegal, undersize lobster; *"They didn't throw the shorts back and got fined for it."*

Slip one's wind: To die; *"She slipped her wind overnight."*

Spleeny: Feeling nervous or anxious about something; *"I'm too spleeny to run right into the lake."*

Sprills: Dropped conifer tree needles; *"The roof's all covered in sprills."*

Stivering: To walk unsteadily; *"She was stivering down the street, so I moved aside."*

Staved, or stoved: To be in disarray, hurt bad, or fundamentally messed up; *"That lawn mower doesn't work; it's all stoved up."*

Supper: (suppah) = Evening meal. Dinner = midday meal that you eat from your dinner pail at work.

Tarter: (tahteh) – An obstinate young child or infant; a youngster being obstinate. In other places they're referred to as "a pistol."

Teeming: Heavy rain; *"It was teeming wicked hard last night."*

The County: Aroostook County, virtually the entire portion of northern Maine, is so vast it is referred to this way. Spelled with a capital T and a capital C.

Tide walkers: A log floating, often with only one end at the surface, in coastal waters; *"A couple of tide walkers collected down in the cove."*

Tipping: To pick fir boughs for wreaths off the tips of conifer branches. *"We went tipping last weekend out in the woods."*

Toteroad: A road through the woods, or a cow path. Once described the trails where logs were "toted" out of the woods.

Well There: *"Well they-ah."* Usually, a response to something being said. Two definitions: the harmless one is like saying, "is that so," or "how about that." Secondly, if someone thinks you're full of it, they'd respond with *"Well there."*

Wicked: Synonym for "very," to a high degree, extremely, exceedingly; *"That steak was wicked good."*

Willie-wacks: WAY out away from civilization. *"Man, you're goin' theah? That's out in the Willie-wacks! One thing for showah – you can't get theah from heah!*

Yard on it: To pull hard; *"Just grab hold and yard on it 'til it comes out."*

Yee yaw: To wiggle something to make it work; *"You've got to yee yaw the lever after you start it up."*

Yow'un: Young person; *"Get those yow'uns out of my toolbox!"*

ABOUT THE AUTHOR

James Reeverts grew up enjoying family vacations to his mother's homestead—a dairy farm in central Maine. Those trips always included the three-hour ride to Seal Harbor on Mount Desert Island's southeastern shore. The proper island relatives they visited would permit recreation only after sitting through afternoon tea with the adults. Traversing the rocky shoreline and swimming at Seal Harbor's beach were much anticipated childhood amusements. But the traditional visit to the shores of Jordan Pond and the restaurant's gift shop held a special fascination. At that time, James had no way of knowing those encounters with the Jordans and the site at Jordan Pond would hold such a captivating influence in later adulthood.

James holds degrees from Spring Arbor University, The State University of New York, and Asbury Theological Seminary. He has served in pastoral roles and spent twenty-five years in public education, teaching science, history, and general education. His family roots go back five generations at Jordan Pond. Jim, as he is known, was selected to the Teacher-Ranger program known as Acadia Teacher Fellows in 2014. He subsequently served as an Education Intern, then an Education Technician, and a Visitor Use Assistant for the National Park Service in Acadia National Park, during the seasons of 2019-2021. During the intervening seasons of 2015-2018, and some years hence, he served the Jordan Pond House at the Guest Services' Information booth. Convinced there is more to the Jordan's story, Jim continues his research and support for the Jordan Pond House and Acadia National Park.

BIBLIOGRAPHY AND REFERENCES

ONLINE:

"1820-1850 a New State & Prosperity." Maine History Online. Accessed April 28, 2018. https://www.mainememory.net/sitebuilder/site/901/page/1312/display.

"Ambajejus - Beautiful and Fascinating." Accessed August 7, 2018. http://penobscotpaddles.blogspot.com/2014/08/ambajejus-beautiful-and-fascinating.html.

Bonesteel, Joyce. "Sawmills Mark the Davis Family's Past." The County Press, accessed August 29, 2018. https://thecountypress.mihomepaper.com/articles/sawmills-mark-the-davis-familys-past/.

"Calm." Passamaquoddy-Maliseet Language Portal, accessed December 5, 2019. https://pmportal.org/taxonomy/term/957.

Dailymail.com. "Black and White Photos Show the Tough Lives of Lumberjacks in the 1800s." Daily Mail Online. Associated Newspapers, accessed December 15, 2015. https://www.dailymail.co.uk/news/article-3360407/Black-white-photos-tough-lives-lumberjacks-+1800s-early-20th-century-massive-trees-fell.html.https://fnai.org/ARROW/almanac/history/history_forestry.cfm.

"Ellsworth, Maine." Wikipedia. Wikimedia Foundation, accessed April 10, 2017. https://en.wikipedia.org/wiki/Ellsworth,_Maine.

Gent, Alan. "Rubber." Tropical Plants, Petroleum, & Natural Gas. Encyclopedia Britannica, Inc. Accessed September 22, 2019. https://www.britannica.com/science/rubber-chemical-compound/Development-of-the-natural- rubber-industry.

"History of the Lumber Industry of America: Defebaugh, James Elliott, 1854- : Free Download, Borrow, and Streaming." Internet Archive. Chicago American

Lumberman, July 1, 1906. Accessed May 12, 2016. https://archive.org/details/historyoflumberi02defeuoft/mode/2up.

Ibach, Marilyn. "Timber-frame Houses in the Historic American Buildings Survey: A Select List." Prints and Photographs Division, Library of Congress. Revised 2003. Accessed April 15, 2021. https://www.loc.gov/rr/print/list/100_tim.html.

"Illegitamate Children and Missing Fathers." genealogy.com. Accessed August 7, 2014. https://www.genealogy.com/articles/research/52_donna.html.

The Jordan Family Foundation. Accessed August 3, 2018. https://thejordanfamilyfoundation.org/.

Katz, Gary, et al. "Hull-Oakes Sawmill." THIS is Carpentry. Accessed March 19, 2016. https://www.thisiscarpentry.com/2011/02/25/hull-oakes-sawmill/.

"Logging in the 1800s." Image galleries, accessed April 9, 2017. https://www.sciencebuzz.org/image/logging_in_the_1800s.

"Loss of Jordan Pond House," *Northeast Harbor Library*, accessed March 6, 2022, https://nehl.digitalarchive.us/items/show/1217. Item 2211.

McKay, Kathryn L. "Trails Of The Past: Historical Overview of the Flathead National Forest, Montana, 1800-1960." US Forest Service. 1994. Accessed April 9, 2017. https://foresthistory.org/wp-content/uploads/2017/01/TRAILS-OF-THE-PAST.pdf.

"Mimuwipon." Passamaquoddy-Maliseet Language Portal, accessed December 5, 2019. https://pmportal.org/dictionary/mimuwipon.

"Moxie Definition & Meaning." Merriam-Webster. Merriam-Webster. Accessed February 17, 2016. https://www.merriam-webster.com/dictionary/moxie.

Neptune, George. "Naming the Dawnland: Wabanaki Place Names on Mount Desert Island." Mount Desert Island Historical Society. Accessed December 5, 2019. https://mdihistory.org/wp-content/uploads/G.NeptuneLayout.pdf.

"The Oregon Encyclopedia, 'logging on big sandy Leona, Oregon, 1889,'" accessed March 6, 2018. https://www.oregonencyclopedia.org/media-collections/timber-industry-1/?grid=1.

Owner, WSD. "A History of Maine Logging." Wood Splitters Direct. Accessed March 7, 2018. https://www.woodsplitterdirect.com/blogs/wsd/a-history-of-maine-logging.

Patterson III, William, and Saunders, Karen E., and Horton, L. J. *Fire Regimes of the Coastal Maine Forests of Acadia National Park*. United States Department of the Interior. National Park Service. North Atlantic Region. Office of Scientific Studies. (OSS 83-3) Digitized version (http://archive.org/details/fireregimesofcoa00patt).

Patterson III, William. 2006. "*The paleoecology of fire and oaks in eastern forests.*" In: Dickinson, Matthew B., ed. 2006. *Fire in eastern oak forests: delivering science to land managers, proceedings of a conference,* 2005 November 15-17; Columbus, OH. (Gen. Tech. Rep. NRS-P-1.) Newtown Square, PA: U.S. Department of Agriculture, Forest Service, Northern Research Station: 2-19. Digitized Version. (http://www.nrs.fs.fed.us/pubs/8429).

"Skagit River Journal." William Entwistle, logger from 1876 onwards. Accessed March 7, 2018. http://www.skagitriverjournal.com/Logging/WAW/Log02-Entwistle1876.html.

"Timber Framing." Wikipedia. Wikimedia Foundation, accessed April 15, 2021. https://en.wikipedia.org/w/index.php?title=Timber_framing&oldid=1017883783.

"Tuberculosis." Mayo Clinic. Mayo Foundation for Medical Education and Research, accessed April 3, 2021. https://www.mayoclinic.org/diseases-conditions/tuberculosis/symptoms-causes/syc-20351250.

"Wikipedians." Wikipedia. Wikimedia Foundation, accessed November 10, 2017. https://en.wikipedia.org/w/index.php?title=American_historic_carpentry&oldid=1+011901696.

Wisconsin Historical Society. "Historic Building Materials and Methods," accessed September 18, 2014. https://www.wisconsinhistory.org/Records/Article/CS4199.

PRINT

"Acadia National Park Resource Management Records, 1854 – 2012 [Bulk Dates 1932-1984]. 'Series VIII: Land Files. Land Deeds: Transferred from JD Rockefeller, Jr. Undated. *Abstract of Title of Land in Mount Desert, Near Jordan's Pond, Hancock County, Maine, Deed 140.*'" Box 132, Folder 6. Department of the Interior. National Park Service. Accessed 7/31/2014.

"Acadia National Park Resource Management Records, 1854 – 2012 [Bulk Dates 1932-1984]. 'Series VIII: Land Files. Land Deeds: Transferred from JD Rockefeller, Jr. Undated. *Abstract of Title of Land Near Jordan Pond, Mount Desert, Maine* (and Supplement) *Deed 141.*'" Box 132, Folder 7. Department of the Interior. National Park Service. Accessed 7/31/2014.

Annonson, A., comp. Jordan, Roland Gene, ed., *The Family Jordan*, vol. 1. Stonington, ME: Penobscot Press. 2001.

Billings, Richard W. *The Village and The Hill*. Augusta, ME: Day Mountain Publishing Company, 1985.

Caldwell, Bill. "Indian Baskets to Steamer Trunks… The Development of Mount Desert Island." *Acadia Weekly*. August 3-9, 2003.

Carter, Lyda B. *Early History of Seal Harbor*. Typescript. Northeast Harbor, ME: Northeast Harbor Library Archives, January 1959.

DeCosta, B.F. *Rambles on Mount Desert: With sketches of Travel on the new-England Coast from Isles of Shoals to Grand Menan*. New York: A.D.F. Randolf & Co., 1871.

Defebaugh, James Elliott. *History of The Lumber Industry of America*. Chicago: The American Lumberman, 1907.

Dodge, Ezra A. *Mount Desert Island and the Cranberry Isles*, Ellsworth, ME: N.K. Sawyer, Printer, 1871.

Dorr, George B. "Acadia, Gathering the Land." *Acadia Weekly*, July 24-30, 2005.

Dorr, George B. "*Notes on acquisition of Land. 'Letter to Mrs. Pine.'*" Box 1 Folder 6. Department of the Interior. National Park Service. Acadia National Park Resource Management Records.

Dorr, George B.. *The Story of Acadia National Park.* 3rd ed. Bar Harbor, ME: Acadia Publishing Co., 1997.

Elliott, Emily Thompson. *A Brief Early Logging History.* Patten, ME: Patten Lumberman's Museum, nd.

Hale, Jr., Richard W. *The Story of Bar Harbor: An Informal History Recording One Hundred and Fifty Years in the Life of a Community.* New York: Ives Washburn, Inc., 1949.

Hancock County Trustees of Public Reservations. *The Hancock County Trustees of Public Reservations: An Historical Sketch, second edition.* Ellsworth, ME: HCTPR, 2016.

Jordan, Charles M. *Jordan Family Descendants.* Decorah, IA: Anunsdsen Publishing Co., 1987.

Jordan, Frank Greely. *The Jordan Family Historical Sketches.* Minneapolis, MN, 1927.

Jordan, John S. "Published Letter to Probate Court." In *Ellsworth American.* Office of Probate Records, 1880.

"Jordan Pond House Burns." *Bangor Daily News,* June 22, 1979; Microfilm Archives, Special Collections Department. Raymond H. Fogler Library, Orono, ME: University of Maine.

Jordan, Tristram Frost, comp. *The Jordan Memorial: Family Records of the Rev. Robert Jordan And His Descendants in America.* Reprinted from 1882. Somersworth, NH: New England History Press, 1982.

McBride, Bunny and Prins, Harald E.L. *Indians in Eden: Wabanakis and Rusticators on Maine's Mount Desert Island 1840s – 1920s.* Camden, ME: Downeast Books, 2009.

McCloskey, Robert. *Burt Dow, Deep-Water Man: A Tale of the Sea in the Classic Tradition*. New York, N.Y.: Puffin Books, 1989.

McIntire, T. A. *The Story of Jordan Pond House* (1915). *Maine History Documents*. 110. https://digitalcommons.library.umaine.edu/mainehistory/110.

Morrison, Samuel Eliot. *The Story of Mount Desert Island*. Boston, MA: Little, Brown & Company, 1960.

Schmitt, Catherine. *Historic Acadia National Park: The Stories behind One of America's Great Treasures*. Guilford, CT: Lyons Press, 2016.

Stebbins, George. *Random notes on the early history and development as a summer resort of Mount Desert Island and particularly Seal Harbor*. Typescript. Seal Harbor, ME: Seal Harbor Library, August 1938.

Street, George E. *Mount Desert A History*. Samuel A. Eliot, ed. Cambridge, MA: The Riverside Press; Boston, MA.: Houghton, Mifflin, and Company, 1905.

Sweetser, M.F. *Chisolm's Mount Desert Guidebook*. Portland, ME: Hugh J. Chisholm, Chisolm Brothers, 1888.

Terrie, Philip G. *Contested Terrain: A New History of Nature and People in the Adirondacks*. Blue Mountain Lake, NY: The Adirondack Museum/Syracuse University Press, 1997.

Watercolor by Thomas J. Reeverts.